BALTIC SOUTHWEST PILOT

BALTIC SOUTHWEST PILOT

Mark Brackenbury
Charts designed and drawn by the author

STANFORD MARITIME · LONDON

Stanford Maritime Limited
Member Company of the George Philip Group
12–14 Long Acre   London WC2E 9LP
Editor Phoebe Mason

First published in Great Britain 1983
Copyright © Mark Brackenbury 1983

Charts designed and drawn by the author
Set in Monophoto Ehrhardt 11/12
by Tameside Filmsetting Limited, Ashton-u-Lyne, Lancashire
Printed in Great Britain
by BAS Printers Limited, Over Wallop, Hampshire

Photographs of Hanklit, Kronborg Castle, Gavnø Castle,
Møns Klint, Stevns Klint and Aaholm Castle are courtesy
of the Danish Tourist Board, London

British Library Cataloguing in Publication Data
Brackenbury, Mark
    Baltic southwest pilot.
    1. Pilot guides—Baltic Sea
    I. Title
    623.89′29163′34   VK819

    ISBN 0-540-07414-4

To C.J.B., V.C.B., P.M. and D.H.G.B.
who all gave up their hard-earned summer holidays to work even harder
helping me to cover the whole area of this book in one season

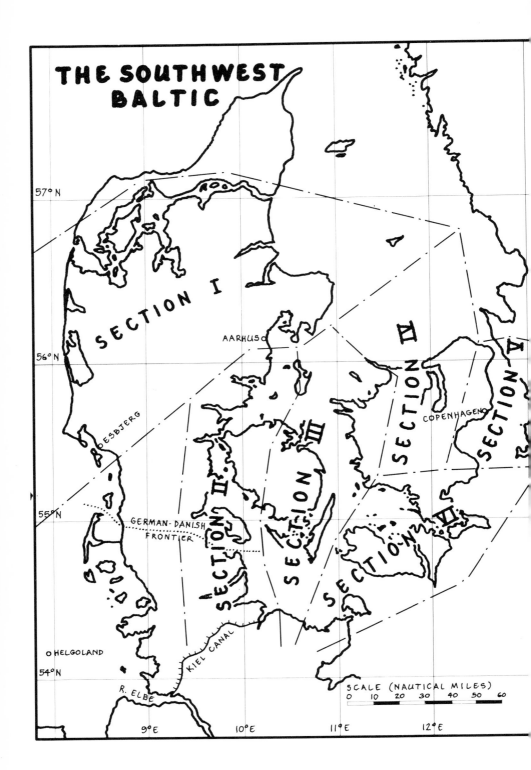

THE SOUTHWEST
BALTIC

57° N

SECTION I

AARHUS

56° N

ESBJERG

SECTION II

SECTION III

SECTION IV

COPENHAGEN

SECTION V

55° N

GERMAN-DANISH
FRONTIER

SECTION

SECTION

SECTION

O HELGOLAND

54° N

KIEL CANAL

R. ELBE

SCALE (NAUTICAL MILES)
0 10 20 30 40 50 60

9° E   10° E   11° E   12° E

Contents

Cruising in the Southwest Baltic

The Baltic is a very large sea, extending eastward to Leningrad and northward almost as far as the Arctic Circle, while to add to the complications inhabitants of the Scandinavian countries do not regard the Baltic proper (Østersoen in Danish) as starting until south and east of the Danish archipelago. Waters north of Sjaelland are referred to as the Kattegat, and the Great and Little Belts and Øresund (the Sound) as the Belt Seas. However, I have adopted western European usage which regards these waters as divisions of the Baltic, hence the title of this book. Apart from a special note on Esbjerg, a useful passage port, the area covered is the Limfjord, and all the waters south and west of a line from Hals at the east end of the Limfjord round the north of Anholt to Hälsingborg in Sweden, and from Skanör (also in Sweden) round the east of the Danish islands and Fehmarn to the German mainland east of Heiligenhafen. This includes all the popular Danish cruising areas except Bornholm, which lies 60 miles to the east of this area, and covers virtually the whole of the West German Baltic coast, together with the Swedish coast of Øresund. It will be found that this book meshes in exactly with my *Norwegian Cruising Guide*, which as well as Norway includes the west Swedish coast as far south as Mölle, only 11 miles or say a couple of hours' sailing from Gilleleje or Hornbaek which are covered in this book. The two guides thus provide continuous coverage from the Sognefjord (north of Bergen) to the Kiel Canal, where my *Frisian Pilot* takes over and continues west and south to Den Helder in the Netherlands.

Contrary to widely held belief, the beautiful and sheltered cruising grounds of the Southwest Baltic are well within reach of an ordinary U.K.-based family cruising boat if a four week holiday is available, or of course the boat can be cruised out one season, left to overwinter and brought back the following year, thus allowing a far more leisurely and detailed exploration of these charming waters. Chartering presents yet another alternative: the Danish Tourist Board, 169 Regent St, London W1 (tel (01) 734 2637) has a list of charter firms, or Danware Ltd, 7 Crispin Way, Farnham Common, Bucks (tel Farnham Common 4562) specialise in package cruising holidays in Denmark, in which the client loads up his car and drives to the picking-up point, crossing by the ferry from Harwich or Newcastle to Esbjerg. This is a good arrangement as the amount of personal gear needed on a cruise is usually a bit more than you can conveniently hump around by public transport.

Before sailing for Denmark, it is well worth visiting or writing to the Danish Tourist Board in London. Make it clear that you are going to be there on a sailing holiday, as they have several booklets and brochures especially for the yachtsman as well as beautifully produced and informative maps and literature on the whole of Denmark and on various regions and smaller areas. When you get there, practically every town and village has its own Tourist Office, where detailed local leaflets are available as well as the more general ones.

Getting There

By way of the Kiel Canal, Copenhagen is 536 miles from Harwich: a fair distance, but possible in a fortnight without any long passages. In fact as long ago as 1969 I moored at Langelinie, the yacht harbour in the centre of Copenhagen, at lunchtime on the thirteenth day after leaving West Mersea, and that was sailing with a boatload of young children, having made only one overnight passage (West Mersea to Ijmuiden and on into the Ijsselmeer), and without pushing at all hard. Having left on the Saturday morning that my holiday began, we were there on the Thursday of the second week, and with a four week holiday we could have stayed until Saturday morning and still had fifteen days to get back. We had logged 686 miles on the outward leg, an average of just over 50 miles a day, but the first $1\frac{1}{2}$ day passage (or a little more: 0415 Saturday to 2045 Sunday) accounted for 200 miles and the average thereafter was only 44 miles a day.

This is the route used by most British yachts, but in fact over the years I have come to favour the Limfjord for the outward passage and the Kiel Canal homeward. The strongly crewed boat can of course save a great deal of time by making straight for Thyborøn, the port at the west end of the Limfjord, a passage of 390 miles from Harwich; or if that is too far for the crew's taste it can be broken in two with little added distance by going Harwich – Terschelling (180 miles), and then Terschelling – Thyborøn (230 miles). Many yachts would hope to make the direct passage in little over three days, and as I have returned from the Baltic to the East Coast in less than a week with only two aboard for most of the way, a tough crew like that would be able to spend thirteen days in the Limfjord and Baltic even with a three week holiday.

Speeds like that are beyond most people's ambition, however, and perhaps a more interesting statistic is that in 1981 my daughter and I reached Thyborøn after only twelve sailing days, along the North Sea coasts and with only one overnight passage. That way we logged 632 miles from Mersea to Thyborøn as compared with about 400 for the direct passage – but we enjoyed every yard of the trip!

Dutch barge-yacht in Augustenborg Fjord

For those with plenty of time the Limfjord route has the advantage of passing through a different and fascinating part of Denmark, and it removes the necessity for retracing your steps for a considerable part of the cruise: going out by Limfjord and home by Kiel, there is no need ever to visit the same port twice during the cruise. I recommend that sequence rather than the reverse, because I think most people will prefer to have the longest passage near the beginning of a cruise, and because most bad weather in summer is likely to be from the west, and so astern or quartering on the long passage across, whereas coming back via Kiel there are all sorts of sheltered inland options if it blows hard from the west.

Even if the crew prefer to keep the passages short, the Limfjord route is still not ruled out: after crossing the North Sea it is easy to coast along to Helgoland by day. After that a second 36 hour passage will reach Thyborøn, or the trip can be broken into two very long day sails, using Esbjerg as a halfway stop. But remember that if it comes on to blow hard from the west the Jutland coast is long and bleak: Esbjerg is a wild and difficult entrance in heavy onshore weather, and Thyborøn should on no account be attempted in onshore gales (see the entries on these ports), so if the weather suddenly takes a turn for the worse the capability must be there to run back for Helgoland, or to continue past Thyborøn and the Limfjord into the Skaggerak, running round into the shelter of the Skaw. But summer gales are not all that common, and it would be bad luck indeed to leave Helgoland with a good forecast and be caught by one before reaching shelter.

For those who plan to day-sail after the first crossing, a list of useful ports, none more than a long day apart, would be Scheveningen, Ijmuiden, Den

Helder (or Oudeschild), Terschelling (or Oost Vlieland), Lauwersoog, Borkum, Norderney, Langeoog (or Spiekeroog), and Helgoland. From the east coast of England one can make Ijmuiden or even Den Helder in 36 hours; south coast sailors may prefer to make the short crossing and go straight along the Belgian and Dutch coasts or even through the Dutch canals if time allows. The navigation of the waters from Den Helder to Helgoland and the Kiel Canal is covered in detail by my *Frisian Pilot* (also published by Stanford Maritime Ltd). Dutch and German charts are much to be preferred for those waters; full details of which are required and where to get them will also be found in that book.

Stores and Supplies

In recent years, the old certainties about relative costs of living have disappeared in a welter of volatile exchange rates, but in general I would say that the only foodstuff that is worth going to some trouble to avoid buying in Denmark is coffee. Otherwise some foods are more expensive, some cheaper, but the differences are not really worth bothering about. Diesel is much more expensive than in England or Germany so it is worth filling up in Helgoland if entering via the Limfjord or in Kiel if via the canal, and trying to judge things so that you get back to Germany with nearly empty tanks. Wine is now cheaper than in the U.K., and beer is reasonable, but spirits are very expensive and it is well worth shipping a bond. Yachts under 40 registered tons have no absolute right to be allowed to ship duty-free stores in the U.K., but in practice H.M. Customs will normally allow this to boats bound beyond the north bank of the Elbe, and it is well worth the trouble. Contact your local Customs office well in advance to get the paperwork tied up, and check up on the regulations with them.

Import allowances into Denmark (1981) were $\frac{3}{4}$ litre spirits, 3 L table wine and 2 L beer, 200 cigarettes (or equivalent) and 750g real coffee or 300g instant per head. Danish rules permit any excess to be bonded in a locker aboard, but be warned that this is not permitted in Sweden, so one should avoid visiting that country carrying excess stores (the allowance there (1981) being 1 L spirits and wine, 2 L beer, and 200 cigarettes). Yachts arriving in Denmark with less than the permitted stores are exempt from Customs clearance: if over, they must proceed as soon as possible to a Customs port (which include Esbjerg, Thisted near the entrance to the Limfjord, or Sønderborg or Rødbyhavn are convenient coming from Kiel) and report themselves. In Sweden also, by the rules in force in 1981, no clearance is required unless the boat has excess stores: if she has they will be taken ashore and can only be reclaimed from the same Customs office during working hours on the day the boat is leaving Sweden, which must be within 30 days in any case. This presents no problem for a single visit to a single Swedish port, as long as it is a Customs port, but is no use for a coastal cruise leaving the country miles from where it was entered. But note that *all these are 1981 regulations, subject to change*, as are the duty-free allowances quoted above.

Equipment and Gear

There are no special problems in the Baltic that require any gear that would not normally be carried on a well-equipped cruising boat. The most usual method of mooring is bow to a jetty and quarter lines to two posts, so it can be useful to carry two boathooks of reasonable length and with good-sized heads, so that a loop of warp can be held out on them and dropped over the posts. Danes hardly ever anchor for the night, and this is a good way to avoid crowded harbours (and keep down the bill for dues!): a Bruce or CQR will hold well in most conditions where anchoring is advisable. In harbours, normal fenders are ample.

One piece of 'special equipment' I did carry on my 1981 cruise, and which amply repaid the trouble, was a folding bicycle. Shops and tourist attractions are often a considerable distance from the harbours, and one or more bicycles can be worth their weight in gold. Mine spent most of its time lashed to the stern pulpit once we were in the Baltic, and came to no harm in spite of going for a swim in Korsør harbour (I hosed it down straight away, but the low salt content of Baltic water was also a help).

Electricity in Denmark is 220V, 50Hz as in the U.K., though the Continental two-pin plugs and sockets are used and thus an adaptor will be necessary.

Finally, I should perhaps mention under this heading that Danish buoys are poor emaciated little things (in sharp contrast to either the human or bovine population!) that can be very difficult to see at any distance. I find that my binoculars get more use in the Baltic than in any other area I know, so it is highly advisable to have a good pair aboard.

Repairs and Accidents

As far as possible, I have mentioned repair facilities under each harbour. Certainly where they are mentioned they exist: there may well be cases where facilities were available that I failed to discover. On the whole Denmark is one of the best countries in Europe to have boat repairs made: in my experience the standard of work is good, everyone falls over themselves to be helpful, and prices are not unreasonable. Remember that work tends to start – and stop – earlier than is usual in England: 8 a.m. is a quite normal starting time. One facility I have *not* mentioned in the text is the existence of a slipway; the reason is that in the almost tideless conditions practically every harbour in the entire country has one.

As far as personal accident or injury is concerned, acute illness or accidental injury is treated free in hospital casualty departments. Employees (including self-employed) and pensioners from EEC countries including Britain are entitled to substantial refunds of pharmacists' and doctors' bills: you should get a Form E 111 from your local Social Security office before leaving home to ensure receiving this benefit. Pharmacists will deduct the refund from the bill, but doctors have to be paid in full and a refund claimed from a local municipal or health service office. Non-qualifying U.K. citizens also receive a more limited refund: the presentation of a British passport is all that is needed to claim this.

Weather

In my experience summer weather in the Danish Baltic is seldom worse than that in southeast England, and often very much better. Temperatures are seldom oppressively high (though I have measured over 80°F in my cabin), but the clear air makes the sun feel warmer on the skin than one is used to in England, and the high latitudes – the area corresponds in latitude roughly with Whitby to Aberdeen – mean that sunshine lasts until late in the evening in the summer months. At Aalborg in the Limfjord, for instance, the sun rises on June 21 at 0425 local time and does not set until 2217. Plenty of time to get a sun-tan! In that northern part of the area darkness lasts for only a couple of hours during June.

Winds tend to blow freely over the generally low-lying land, and the yachtsman does not suffer nearly so much from funnelling and wind-shadows as he does in other Scandinavian countries. Wind directions are predominantly westerly in summer, with July figures in the south of our region recording 61 per cent of winds between SW and NW, compared with 26 per cent between NE and SE. The same station (Fehmarnbelt Lt V) recorded 3 per cent calms in July, 50 per cent force 1–3, 33 per cent force 4–5, and 13 per cent force 6–7, which leaves only 1 per cent for the real nasties!

Tides, Currents and Depths

The tidal rise and fall is really only perceptible in certain areas: the maximum mean range is 1.5m, found along the S coast of Falster and Lolland, but $\frac{1}{4}$–$\frac{1}{2}$m is more usual. Even this is enough to cause perceptible tidal streams in calm weather, but with established winds the wind-driven currents are usually stronger than the tidal streams. The strongest currents occur in the three great channels that link the Kattegat to the Baltic proper. In strong north winds currents in the Little and Great Belts are south-going, but that in the Sound is north-going. In strong easterlies and southerlies all are north-going, and in strong westerlies all are south-going. The strongest streams are found in the north part of the Sound between Helsingør (Elsinore) and Hälsingborg, where the south-going current in westerlies and the north-going one in easterlies can reach 3 knots. But the fact that the currents are south-going in the prevailing westerly wind adds to the advantage of the 'out by the Limfjord, home by Kiel' cruise plan. The general current in the Limfjord is usually east-going in summer.

And now for a vitally **Important Note**. All charts of the Baltic from whatever nation are based on a Chart Datum of Mean Sea Level. This means that *at low tide* under average meteorological conditions, *there will be less water than charted*. Far more important is the fact that wind effects can raise or lower the level at half-tide by anything up to 1.5 metres above and below the mean. Where this may be critical in the case of shallow harbours I have mentioned it in the text, but it must always be remembered that, in contrast to charts of the Channel and North Sea, for instance, there may well be *substantially less water than shown on the chart*. A level of a metre below datum would be rare in summer, except in strongly tidal areas like South Lolland, where LW springs already gives a level almost a metre below ML. But wind effects can easily produce a rise or fall of $\frac{1}{2}$ metre from ML, over and above the tide. This seldom matters in the open sea, where there is usually ample water for a yacht as long as nobody is trying any clever short-cuts: the real danger is in the shallower harbours. *Never* spend a night in a harbour where the charted depth (always given on the chart beside the harbour's name) is not at least $\frac{1}{2}$ metre more than your draft. There may well be more water than charted when you enter, but a change of wind could leave you neaped, and stuck there until the next time the wind brings the extra water back. I remember years ago meeting an English yachtsman who was highly pleased with himself for getting his boat, drawing 6ft, into a harbour 'supposed to have only $1\frac{1}{2}$ metres, old boy!' I explained the above facts to him, and we hurried back to the harbour, where he had been since the previous evening. Sure enough, he was hard aground. By dint of heeling his boat by hauling on a line to her masthead we got him out, but it was a close thing, and by later that day the water was down another 6 inches: if he had still been there, it would have been 'for the duration'.

Charts and Pilot Books

British Admiralty charts give very much better coverage of the area than they did some years ago, but in the nature of things they must be less up to date than the official Danish ones, or German where applicable, so on the whole I recommend the use of local charts. The Danish ones are in fact cheaper than the British, as long as they are bought in Denmark, and as they are widely available there I suggest getting only the necessary minimum before arrival and buying the rest in Denmark as needed. This also has the advantage that if one's plans are changed, unnecessary charts are not paid for and then never used. Danish charts can be obtained in the U.K. through J. D. Potter, 145 Minories, London EC3, tel (01) 709 9076. Also by mail from Iver Weilbach & Co., Toldbodgade 35, P.O. Box 2051, DK-1253 Copenhagen K, Denmark; this firm is a chart agent and a nautical instrument and book shop.

If going via the Limfjord only Danish chart 104 need be on board, with the first local batch being bought at Nykøbing Mors or Lemvig. If from the Kiel Canal 185 is the basic, plus 154 if bound for Sønderborg and the Little Belt, 170 for Marstal and the Great Belt, or 186 if bound direct for the Sound (Øresund) and Copenhagen, when they could be bought at Rødby Havn. The diagrams of Danish chart coverage printed with this section show the areas covered: for greater clarity I have omitted the very large-scale ones that I do not consider will ever be needed by yachts.

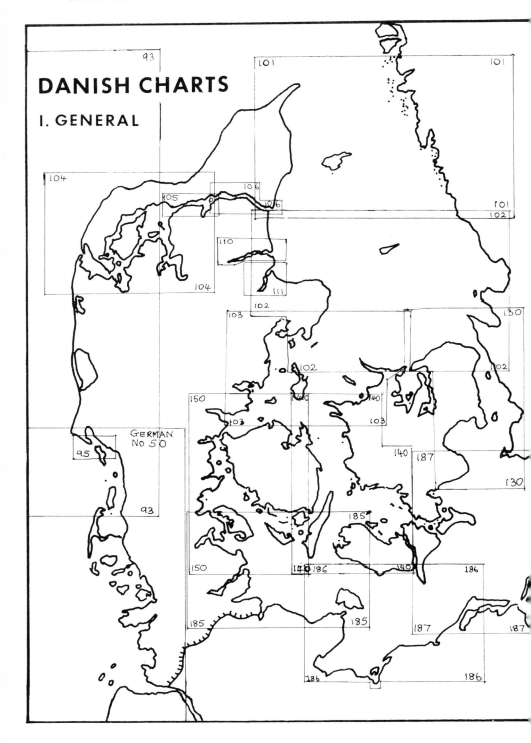

DANISH CHARTS

I. GENERAL

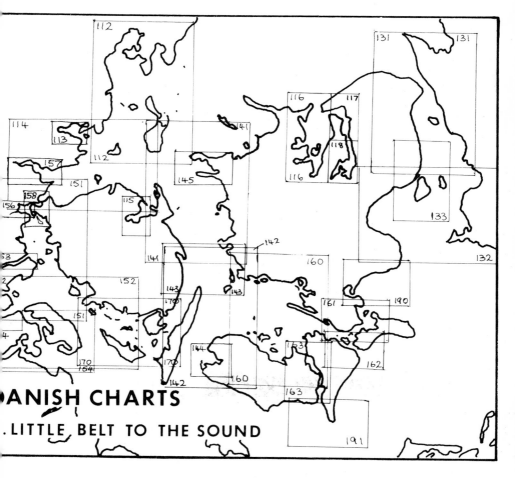

DANISH CHARTS

LITTLE BELT TO THE SOUND

As the Danish charts are cheaper than the German ones and at least as good, I do not recommend the use of the latter except when exploring the Schlei, which is not covered in the Danish series. From Dan Helder to Brunsbüttel and as far as Helgoland, detailed advice on charts is to be found in my *Frisian Pilot*: for the west Jutland coast German 50 and Danish 93 are ample, in conjunction with the plan of Esbjerg in this book. Thyborøn is covered amply by plans on Danish 104, mentioned above.

Just before this book was printed a new series of Baltic charts became available in Britain. Heinemann's Sportschiffsfahrkarten (yachting charts) are based on German Admiralty charts and cover the SW Baltic in three sets: *A* – Round Fyn to Kiel Bay (13 charts), *B* – Lübecker Bay to Bornholm, South Zeeland to Copenhagen (15 charts), and *C* – Samsø Belt and the Kattegat (8 charts). They provide all the necessary harbour plans, and are very good value for the coverage. There is also *D* – The Schlei (2 charts), but it seems to offer no advantage over the excellent German

Admiralty charts mentioned in the text. Available in the U.K. from Imrays, Wych House, The Broadway, St Ives, Huntingdon PE17 4BT.

In my choice of plans to illustrate this book I have assumed that the reader will be using Danish charts, and so I have omitted plans where there is a satisfactory large-scale inset of a particular harbour on the appropriate Danish chart. I have also omitted plans where the harbour is simply a small square or circular basin between piers, or where it is sufficiently shown on the working part of the chart, some of which are on quite a large scale. Plans here have therefore been restricted to those harbours that are not properly shown on the chart, and where the layout is complex enough to make a plan of some real value; unnecessary ones would only have added to the cost and therefore the price of the book. In most cases the equivalent British Admiralty chart will have the same inset as the Danish chart from which it is derived. All chart numbers given in the text refer to Danish charts unless otherwise stated.

Finally, if any reader notices new developments, changes or mistakes, particularly in matters of navigational importance, I would be most grateful for a note care of the Editor, Stanford Maritime Ltd, 12–14 Long Acre, London WC2E 9LP.

Turning to pilot books, I have attempted to make this one comprehensive enough to avoid the actual need for any other, but for the reasons given above it has not been possible to print plans of every port and harbour covered, whereas virtually every harbour in Denmark has a plan in *Den Danske Havnelods*, the official Danish Pilot. This can also be obtained through Potters, but like the charts is a good deal cheaper if bought locally. The Deutscher Segler-Verband's *Hafenhandbuch Ostsee (Band I)* also has numerous plans, and the advantage of covering German ports too. It has useful information on facilities, but offers no advice (navigational or otherwise) or descriptions.

Scandinavian alphabets

Having raised the question of pilot books and other works which may have an alphabetical index (*Den Danske Havnelods* actually lists all the harbours in alphabetical rather than geographical order), it is important to point out that the Scandinavian alphabets are different from those of the rest of Europe. Z does not occur except in foreign-derived words, and the last three letters are **ae** (written ä in Sweden), **ø** (written ö in Sweden), and å, sometimes still written in the old form **aa** in Denmark. I find that non-Scandinavian readers have great difficulty in coping with this, not so much when the extra letters occur at the beginning of words as when they come in the middle. Just to illustrate the problem, here is an alphabetical list taken from the index of one of my Danish reference books and cut down just to a few relevant names: Skagen, Skive, Skovshoved, Skutholmen, Skælskør, Skødshoved, Skaaninge. **Aa** is, you will note, alphabetised as one letter even when written as two: in most books that last-named harbour would be written Skåninge.

This can cause a great deal of delay and frustration to unaccustomed users, so as in my *Norwegian Cruising Guide*, I have anglicised the system. To avoid the confusion between å and aa, I have used the (old-fashioned) spelling aa throughout (except for the Swedish port of Råå, which would otherwise come out Raaaa), and I have treated (and spelled) ae as ae, and treated ø and ö as o. This does not produce any problems when using a Danish book, as ae never occurs except in its diphthongal form, and aa and å are treated as identical in Scandinavian printing. To preserve the simplicity of the system, the Swedish ä has been treated as a: remember that in Scandinavian lists this letter is grouped together with ae rather than a.

Layout of this Book

It is difficult to find a logical sequence in which to treat a more or less square-shaped area full of irregular islands, but I rejected alphabetical treatment in favour of geographical, because I feel that the reader wants to have the alternative ports he may visit today laid out close together in the book, not scattered through it at random. For the same reason I have dealt with the ports on either side of each major channel in the order they would come abeam when sailing up that channel, as most of the channels are narrow enough to make it irrelevant which side one pulls into to stay the night. There are still bound to be anomalies where one possible port comes in one section and another in another, but I hope the overall cruise-planning chart at the beginning of the book, together with the more detailed ones at the start of Sections I, II and IV, will prevent any problems from arising.

As I suggest entrance via the Limfjord, I have dealt with it, Esbjerg and the Kattegat down to Aarhus as Section I. Section II is from Kiel northwards up the Little Belt and Samsø Belt to Tunø and Norsminde. III goes northwards through the Great Belt to Sjaellands Odde; Section IV eastwards along North Sjaelland to Gilleleje, taking in the Isefjord and Roskildefjord. Section V brings us back southwards through the Sound as far as Stevns Klint, while Section VI deals with the south coast of Sjaelland and the islands to its south, and takes in one or two of the principal harbours on the German mainland east of the Kiel Fjord. The maps make the exact extent of each section clear.

General Notes

I will complete this introduction with some miscellaneous information and advice about cruising the Baltic.

Do remember that in these virtually tideless waters marine toilets should never be used in harbours or confined anchorages. Almost all ports provide excellent toilet facilities: details appear in the text. Similarly, garbage should never be thrown over the side, except for such scraps as are, to use the modern phrase, totally bio-degradeable. Again, almost every port has bins for rubbish available to its users.

Fish stakes are a common phenomenon which the visitor may never have met before. Nets are spread between them, sometimes below the surface. Never sail between these stakes except where there is a gap: narrow gaps in very long lines of stakes are marked by a brush or can marker on the top of the stake at either side of the gap. These things can be a terrible nuisance, but they do have their advantages: almost every shoal in otherwise deep water will be festooned with stakes, which often serve as a much better warning than the rather skinny buoys that are the official markers.

Swing bridges are met in many parts of the area. Throughout Denmark the correct signal to request passage is International Code flag **N** in the rigging (on the signal halyard is usual) and N (–·) sounded on the horn. A national ensign may be used instead of flag N, if necessary, but I think it looks rather messy. Many bridges only open at fixed times: details will be found in the text, under Passage Notes or the port concerned. In summer bridges do not open after dark, certainly for pleasure craft. N should not be flown continuously by boats with no intention of passing through a bridge: this bad habit is rife among local yachtsmen.

Vacant berths in marinas and areas of harbours reserved for yachts are marked by green cards, usually plainly visible while under way, fixed to the jetty about where the bow of the boat will lie when moored. This is an excellent system: each berth has a holder and a plastic card, green on one side, red the other; on leaving for more than a day-sail the berth owner will just place the card with its green side outwards. Often the expected date of return is written on the card. Danish yachtsmen on the whole follow this system meticulously, so it is not only bad form but also asking for trouble to take a berth showing a red card unless advised by a harbourmaster or reliable-looking local person. In just one or two places the cards are circular,

Praestø fjord: eel nets and skinny buoys

Typical eel nets in open water

half green and half red: there it is the colour that is uppermost that counts. This arrangement works extremely well: I only wish we could get something like it going in the U.K.

Weather forecasts are broadcast in English by Radio Denmark (Programme 3) at the end of the News in English at 0815, but they are pretty basic. Much fuller reports are available from coastal radio on VHF, and I find that a good transistor radio will pick up BBC Radio 4 anywhere in the whole area, even the Swedish Sound: the shipping forecast does not cover the Baltic, but the general synopsis is invaluable for building up a picture of future probabilities. Local forecasts in Danish are very difficult to understand, but a friendly Danish neighbour will often oblige with a translation.

Talking of VHF, a word of warning. The VHF channels used as marine working frequencies in Denmark are quite different from those mostly in use in the rest of Europe, so owners whose sets have only a limited number of channels will be well advised to consider having some crystals changed. The whole area is covered by Channels 1, 2, 3, 5, 7, 23, 28 and 65, but of these Ch 1 and 65 can be omitted without too much risk, as losing these two only produces two small blind spots, one (65) north of NW Fyn and the other (1) round the NE corner of Sjaelland, neither more than two or three hours' sail across.

VHF provides one method of communication with home: I also found the public telephone system very efficient. There are no operators, and reversed charges calls are not available, but a single *krone* in the slot gives enough time to report the number of your booth (stuck on the instructions plate in Dymo tape usually, not on the telephone), after which home, office or whoever can ring straight back at the low STD rates.

Harbour dues vary widely. I have given 1981 figures because, although they will almost certainly increase, they will probably remain in proportion and such facts as the length at which a major increase is levied will very likely remain unchanged.

Finally, a word about language. Many Danes speak excellent English, and in emergency teenaged children can almost always help out. In my experience the answer to 'Do you speak English?' is almost always '*Nej*' (No), and it is usually better to plunge straight in and ask your question: many people who would have denied it if asked find they do remember their English when they hear it spoken. On the whole, the farther from Copenhagen the more likely you are to find linguistic problems. But there is one special additional problem that can be quite confusing, which arises from the difficulty of pronouncing Danish in general, and Danish names in particular. This is that even Danes who speak near-perfect English may be quite unable to understand your pronunciation of what seems a perfectly simple name. I read Danish with some facility (as long as the subject is sailing, where all my vocabulary lies!) and even understand it a little when spoken; and yet only a couple of days ago I was talking on the telephone to a Danish friend who speaks perfect English, and when I mentioned Køge he could not understand where I meant until I spelt it. Once he did understand, he repeated the name in a way that was indistinguishable to my ears from what I had been saying. So when enquiring about places, always be ready to write the name down. But don't worry: most people do speak at least a bit of English (or German, if you speak it, can often help out), and struggling with languages is all part of the fun of cruising abroad, anyway!

I · Esbjerg, the Limfjord and Jutland ports to Aarhus including Anholt

Esbjerg
see plan

It may seem odd that the first port dealt with in a book about the Baltic should be on the North Sea, but Esbjerg is a valuable staging-point on the way to the Baltic so it seemed worth including. The plan provided here should enable entry to be made in good conditions, but anyone attempting to make this difficult entrance in bad weather would be well advised to carry the large-scale Danish chart 95, or the British Admiralty equivalent 417.

Esbjerg is a ferry and fishing harbour, lying at the head of the Graadyb, a deep-water channel that runs between the island of Fanø and the Skallingen peninsula. The channel is dredged to a least depth at MLWS of 8.8m, but it is most important to note that depths shoal very rapidly outside the buoyed channel, especially in the region of the dogleg caused by the Tørre Bjaelke shoal. When I visited the harbour in 1981 the still brightly painted wrecks of two British trawlers were visible as a reminder, lying only a matter of a few feet outside the line of buoyage: one had suffered engine failure and the other was attempting a tow when both went aground and quickly broke up.

In spite of the modest tidal range (1.7m at springs and HW Esbjerg is about 3 hours later than HW Dover) tidal streams can exceed 2 knots in the entrance and approach channel, and a SW wind can speed up the flood and slow the ebb. In strong SW winds the entrance can be very rough all the way from No. 1 buoy to the Jerg beacon, a distance of 5 miles which, I assure you, can seem a good deal longer. Conditions in such circumstances are worse during the ebb, and also have to be suffered for longer, because of the foul stream.

Approaching from the S it is safe to steer for buoys 3 and 4 when they are identified, and then proceed up the channel keeping well to the starboard side. At night in rough weather the magnificent leading lights, first pair Iso W, second pair FG, third pair FR, are bright and easy to identify, and it is safer to use them than to try to spot the channel buoys. Beware tidal cross-sets in the outer approach channel.

It is worth remembering that the tall chimneys and silos near the port are clearly visible for over 10 miles in good visibility: from the S an offing of 3 miles from the visible land should be maintained until these bear about 80°

23

CRUISE-PLANNING CHART
SECTION I

SCALE (NAUTICAL MILES)
0   10   20   30   40   50

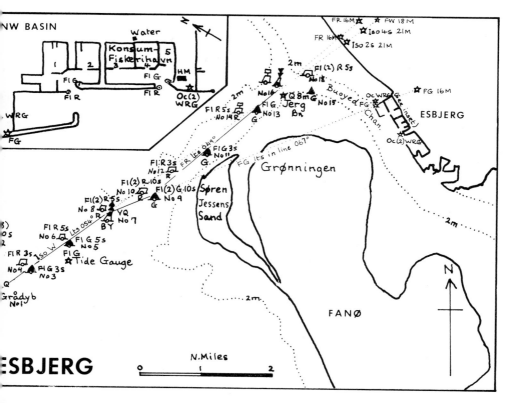

ESBJERG

Mag., when the first pair of channel buoys (N Card., Q and R can, Fl(3) R 10s) should be visible. The Tide Gauge ¼ mile S of No. 5 buoy is also a good landmark, and in light weather it is safe for shallow draft boats to pass close W of it and then cut into the channel to the N, as long as the boat is kept at least 2 cables W of buoy No. 5 until well into the buoyed channel. This short-cut carries 2m at MLWS.

There are no special berths in Esbjerg for visiting yachts: the harbour office keeps a 24-hour watch on Ch 16 and boats with VHF should radio for advice. Otherwise, enter the Konsumfiskerihavn and moor temporarily, walking round to the harbour master's office at the head of the pier by the Oc(2) WRG light. The office is reached by walking through the fish auction hall. A diesel barge operates around the Fiskerihavn on weekdays and Saturday mornings. Water can be taken from a blue box like a small telephone box at the NW corner of basin 2, the middle basin of the Konsumfiskerihavn.

The town centre is a fair walk from the harbour, and no great shakes when you get there, although there are good shops. Beware the misuse of the word 'restaurant': in this part of Denmark, and through most of the Limfjord, many places dignified with this title turn out to be rather sleazy bars that

There are no special moorings in Esbjerg for visiting yachts

often seem to be unable to rustle up so much as a sandwich. Some of the ones near Esbjerg harbour are particularly depressing, and certainly not suitable for ladies or children.

Passage notes – Helgoland to Thyborøn

The southern part of the passage, as far as Esbjerg, presents no special problems, although the navigator must be aware of the dangers of being caught in this area by severe westerly weather. The fishing harbours of the North Frisian islands offer no shelter to the stranger in onshore gales, and if caught by a really bad westerly gale one would have no choice except to run back for Helgoland, which is at least safe to enter in any weather, or on for Esbjerg, which would be a dangerous choice for any but a really heavy and powerful boat in such conditions. Fortunately, however, the BBC's Shipping Forecasts are pretty reliable for this area, and the chance of being caught by quite unexpected bad weather is very small.

Just a few miles N of Esbjerg, the Horns Rev shoal extends offshore for no less than 20 miles from the point of Blaavandshuk, but there is a well-buoyed channel through it only 5 miles out from the land. It is not necessary for a yacht to use the main Slugen channel: at the third green buoy one can turn NW for the red buoy marking Søren Bovbjerg Dyb, and thence steer into open water, saving some 3 miles compared with keeping in the Vestslugen. However, the former channel should not be used in heavy weather as there is an unmarked shallow patch with only 3.7m on it. There is also an inshore channel, steering N from halfway between green buoys Nos. 1 and 2 for a yellow buoy, and then NNE to leave another yellow buoy to port. I have done this, but it is tricky and should only be attempted by an experienced skipper in calm weather.

North of Horn's Rev the shore is steep-to all the way to Thyborøn, and one can keep close in in good weather and benefit from the landmark beacons at intervals along the shore, clearly shown on the Danish chart. There is a considerable harbour at Hvide Sande, some 33 miles N of Esbjerg, which can be used in emergency: beware strong and unpredictable streams in the entrance and harbour. There is an electricity cable across the entrance, clearance 29m.

Thyborøn
see insets on chart 104

This harbour at the W end of the Limfjord has a steep shingle bar which, while leaving ample water for any yacht (there is over 6m in the approach channel) causes dangerous sea conditions in winds over force 6 from between SW and N. The wind also baffles in the approach channel, so if conditions are marginal it is safer to enter under power with sail off. In other conditions the harbour is perfectly safe: I have entered in a southerly gale with no trouble at all.

The approach channel is well buoyed, and at night two sets of leading lights lead into the sheltered inner waters E of the harbour. The entrance is towards the S end of the long E-facing mole, and the lights are not very bright viewed from the N, but the mole itself is well lit by working lights so it is easy enough to run down 100m off shore until the entrance is abeam.

Turning in, a possible strong cross-set must be allowed for. The normal tidal stream runs at 1–2 knots, but in established strong winds this is replaced by a wind-induced current which can reach 6–8 knots, and run unchanged for several days.

There are no specific berths for visiting yachts. The Nordre Inderhavn (the northernmost basin of all) is the best bet: berth alongside as space permits. It has clean but graffitic loos on its W side. The harbour office (open 9–12 and 1.30–3) is 100m further S in a buff-coloured building overlooking the Baadehavn; Customs another 50m S. Rubbish bins beside the loo building. No harbour dues (1981).

The town has modest shops and a sailmaker, Jens Kristian Mikkelsen at Svanegade 14, who will do simple repairs while you wait and at very reasonable cost. In strong SW to NW winds sand blows everywhere in the town and harbour, and winches and other mechanical gadgets should be covered.

The Snail House at the SW corner of the town about 1½ miles from the harbour is an interesting curiosity, decorated with snailshells from all over

Force 9 in Thybor∮n

Thybor∮n entrance, force 9

Hanklint, a 213ft cliff on the N coast of Mors, SE of Thisted. It is composed of diatomaceous earth, with strata of volcanic ash which show the distortions the seabed has undergone.

the world. The 20km railway trip to Strande (Victoria Street!) and back gives a fascinating glimpse of the lakes, lagoons and beaches of the area: the trip takes about an hour.

Passage notes – Thyborøn to Løgstør

Bear in mind that there may be considerable current in the narrower parts of the Limfjord: fortunately this is usually east-going in summer and so helps you on your way. The first 4 miles of the passage lie along the Saelhundeholm Løb, a narrow channel through shifting sandbanks but well buoyed. Once out of the channel, Lemvig lies to the S and Agger (an out-of-the-way spot which I confess I have never visited) to the N. If bound beyond Lemvig, steer no more than 115° to avoid the shoals off the approaches to that port, and cross down to the SE corner of the Nissum Bredning (literally 'Broad'). Here a narrow strait is spanned by a swing bridge: see the introduction above for signals. It opens on demand. The opening section is between piers 3 and 4, counting from the W and when closed clearance is 5m in the centre. This is the Oddesund: once through, Struer lies to the S.

Now the routes to the E divide. The most direct is to pass S and E of the big island of Mors, under Salling Sund bridge (clearance 26m), past the port of Nykøbing Mors, and out into the Løgstør Bredning. More interesting and beautiful, however, is the route round the E side of Jegindø and N through islands and sounds to Thisted (another swing bridge 4½ miles short of there), E through a narrowing sound and then out into the Løgstør

Bredning. This broad contains the lovely islands of Fur and Livø which must not be missed, and fjords to the S, one leading to the major yachting port of Skive. To the E, across the broad, a buoy has to be found which marks the outer end of the channel that leads through the sandbanks to Løgstør.

Lemvig
see inset on chart 104

One of the prettiest towns in West Limfjord, and many people sail straight past Thyborøn and make it their first port of call.

The main approach is on $243\frac{1}{2}°$ Mag. on two leading beacons 2 miles N of

Approaching Lemvig on the leading line

Nykøbing Mors

30

the town; but from the W a course of 140° Mag. from the Saelhunde Løb buoy leads in 3 miles to a green buoy with N cone topmark, from which a course of 180° Mag. leads to a similar buoy in the entrance channel. Stay on the leading line until the second pair of beacons in the town itself come into view.

Visitors can berth in the new marina a mile N of the town on the W side of the fjord. Green card system, no harbourmaster or fuel, but water on the jetties. No supplies nearer than town, but occasional snackbar. I prefer the old harbour where yachts lie bows to the N wall of the Fiskerihavn, stern to posts, or as space allows. Diesel from the Esso pump at E end of basin. Neither harbour charged dues in 1981. The town is most attractive, with good shops, restaurants etc, and rail connections. Nice twelfth century church with a rich Baroque interior.

Struer
see inset on chart 104

The town is called Holsterbro-Struer in Danish Pilots and elsewhere, though the locals cannot understand why! Struer is in fact the port for Holsterbro, which lies 5 miles to the S. Approach is by a narrow buoyed channel.

There are two yacht harbours, one in the W part of the main harbour, and the other a separate two-part basin with its own entrance further W. The town is hidden behind a railway embankment, through a small arch. Good shops, good train service to Esbjerg. Club with showers (cheap), launderette, good loos, food and bar. Diesel in cans only. Good chandler who will do some repairs. Unattractive town, rather industrial and gloomy. No dues in 1981.

Nykøbing, Mors
see inset on chart 104

The identification is needed to avoid confusion with two other Nykøbings. Approached by a long buoyed channel (see inset): there is a yacht harbour immediately to port round the end of the W mole, which can be rough in strong winds. I prefer the NW basin of the Fiskerihavn, just below the harbour office and nearer the shops. Free showers, loos etc at office (open 0800–2200) and at yacht club at W end of marina (24 hr). Diesel pump in NW corner of Fiskerihavn, service from shop (*købmand*) visible to the N. Good chandler near yacht club with a small sail loft. The owner, Leo Sørensen, speaks good English, as does the HM, who used to sail out of Goole. Good shops. Dues Kr20 in 1981.

Dover Odde

This enchanting little jetty harbour is on the route W of Mors. Perfect shelter except in winds from S to E. Water on the pier and on the pontoon projecting S from it, diesel from an incredible old rusty hand-pumped tank: the bar manager, who is also the HM, will operate. Small shop. Dues Kr20 in 1981.

31

Dover Odde. As is common practice, the yachts are moored between pairs of posts and a jetty.

Thisted. The silo (right) makes a good landmark; the yacht club (pale roof) is at the left of the picture.

Thisted
see inset on chart 104

The entrance lies just W of an enormous white silo, a useful landmark when approaching from the S. Coming from the E, ignore the cement works harbour ¾ mile E of the real one.

The entrance can be difficult to make out in hazy conditions, and it is possible to find oneself right on top of the harbour before realising how close it is.

The yacht harbour is immediately to port after entering: diesel is available alongside from the fuel jetty there. Showers and loos in the harbour office, loos and phone also at yacht club just W of main entrance. Good train service to Esbjerg. Largish, dullish town; good shops but about 400m away. Dues (1981) Kr20.

Fur
see plan

A beautiful island and one place in the Limfjord that should not be missed. The small harbour is not well shown on Danish chart 104: it lies $\frac{1}{2}$ mile NE of the southernmost point of the island. Berth (bow and posts) inside the outer breakwater or as space allows. Diesel in cans only; the quayside pump is for large amounts only. For facilities see plan: the loos are in a low grey blockhouse that looks unpromising. The restaurant in the *kro* opens 11–2 and 4–8. Dues Kr20 in 1981.

The shopping is no great shakes, but the island is very beautiful, and it is well worth hiring bicycles and exploring.

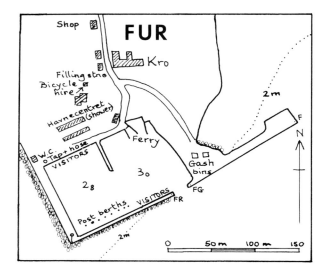

Ferry leaving Fur

33

Livø
see plan

The harbour lies on the E side of this tadpole-shaped island, and has room for only six or eight boats: the S outer jetty is reserved for the ferry, but a couple of additional short-term berths can be found along the S side of the N outer jetty.

Approaching from W or S, beware of the shoal continuing the tadpole's tail: its end is marked by an unlit E Cardinal buoy. The rust-coloured shelter for ferry passengers with bright green roof is a good landmark from all sides: the entrance itself can only be seen from fairly close inshore to the S. Crowded at weekends and in the holiday season. There is 2.5m in the harbour, but this can fall by 1m in strong NE winds.

The island is very beautiful, with masses of wild roses and woods. There is a small shop and cafeteria in the 'village', which was in fact built as an asylum for the criminally insane for the whole of Denmark. When I was there the whole island was full of children, taken there in school parties, sleeping in the old buildings, and having a perfectly marvellous time. Definitely not to be missed. Dues (1981) Kr20.

Shop hours 8–12.30 and 4–4.30: cafeteria 8 a.m.–11 p.m. The harbour has no facilities except toilets – grass-roofed!

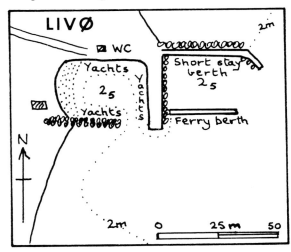

Hvalpsund
see plan

A useful yacht harbour about 10 miles S of Livø, on the way to Skive. It is a large, modern marina, with slip, crane, fuel and all facilities. It is not properly named on the chart, but is the more northerly of the two harbours shown on the E side of Hvalp Sund at about 56° 42½′N. The approach is straightforward as long as care is taken to keep well east of Rotholm Rev, the long shoal running N from Rotholm, which is well buoyed. There is 1m range at mean tides, and E–SE winds can lower the mean level by up to 1m.

Dues (1981) Kr20. Diesel available at the Fiskerihavn, ½ mile to the SW.

Livø harbour

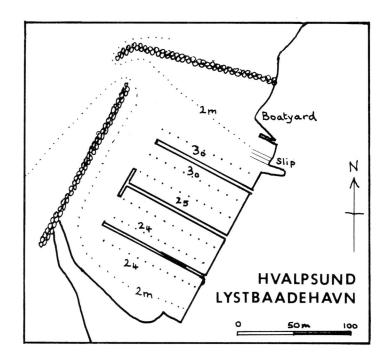

Skive

see inset on chart 104

This is a considerable but not very interesting town, mainly worth visiting as the major port for substantial boat repairs in the area, for which Skive Baadbyggeri Kaare-Weber should be contacted. The approach down Skive Fjord requires care: there are two long shoals projecting from Lundø, of which the more southerly extends fully halfway across the fjord. S of this all is clear, and yachts can (and should) keep out of the buoyed narrow approach channel, which is dredged to 4.1m and only needed by deep-draft commercial vessels: the rest of the fjord has at least 2.4m.

The yacht harbour (2.5m within the buoyed area) lies N of the commercial basins; yachts over 40ft should use the Nordhavn. No dues were payable in 1981. All facilities, but the town and shops involve a fair walk. The old church has beautiful frescoes. It is unsafe to go out at night: the human inhabitants are law-abiding and charming, but the mosquitoes are savage!

Løgstør

see inset on chart 105

Approaching from the W or S, the offing buoy (red can, Fl(3) R 10s) which lies 4 miles NNE of the N point of Livø must be identified, and the narrow buoyed channel then followed through the shoals. (Until the channel was dredged there was no passage except by the Frederik VII canal which still forms part of Løgstør harbour.) Yachts berth in the Østre Kanalhavn or the Fiskerihavn as space allows.

There is water on the Fiskerihavn quay, a small shop between the two harbours, and a diesel pump on the mainland side of the Kanalhavn, served from the shop. Loos and showers. Dues (1981) Kr15.

The town, about 200m E from the Fiskerihavn, is charming, with a huge greenhouse full of flowers in the centre and numerous good shops. Some streets of old fishermen's houses are preserved, and well worth a visit.

Løgstør: the entrances to both basins can be seen

Passage notes – Løgstør to Hals and the Baltic

This eastern half of the Limfjord has a quite different character from the wide waters of the western part. As far as Aalborg the fjord varies in width from 1 to over 5 miles, but the channel (which is well buoyed) is only from 2 cables to 100 yards or less wide. E of Aalborg the fjord narrows to a width of half a mile to a mile, but the channel is if anything wider and less tricky to follow.

Leaving Løgstør, we soon reach the Aggersund lifting bridge which opens on demand (usual signals). Three miles farther on the channel to Attrup branches off to port and then the fjord widens out into the Nibe Bredning. At the E side of this is a shallow bar with a narrow dredged channel (Draget) which must be followed with care. From here the buoyed channel leads to Aalborg. Just to the W of the town the word *Afmaerkingenskifte* is printed across the channel on the chart: here the direction of lateral buoyage changes. From here we are going down to the Baltic and leave green buoys to port, not coming up from the North Sea leaving them to starboard.

The yacht harbour at Aalborg is W of the bridges, which need careful timing. Both open 0500 to 2100, but the road bridge is closed on weekdays from 0640–0710, 0740–0810, 0840–0910, 1150–1220, 1240–1310, 1540–1630 and 1650–1730. On Saturdays, the first three closures apply plus 1130–1230. Sundays (June 20–Aug 15) closed 1600–1630, 1700–1730 and 1800–1830. Signals from the bridge: 1 FR means 'wait'; 2 Fl R, E–W traffic prepare; 2 FR, E–W go; 3 Fl R, W–E prepare; 3 FR, W–E go. Usual signals for requesting passage through.

It is worth noting that E of Aalborg there is a shallower channel which still has 4m rounding the first bend: it is marked by smaller red buoys with topmarks and saves a little distance. It is particularly useful if the current is foul, as the stream is weaker out of the deep channel. Otherwise the passage to Hals is straightforward. From Hals to the open Baltic the channel passes through shoals and it must be followed carefully, although it is safe for an average-sized yacht to turn S or N without bothering to pass through the last two pairs of channel buoys.

Attrup
see plan

This friendly little yacht harbour lies on the N bank of the fjord about 6 miles E of the Aggersund bridge. The main channel is left when N of the more westerly beacon on Marbjerg Tunge, from where the fluorescent pink spherical offing buoy (not yellow with topmark as charted) will be seen to the NNW. From this buoy turn ENE, and the small but numerous channel buoys will be seen. This would be a tricky approach in poor visibility.

Enter on the leading line (see sketch chart) and berth as space allows. Water and electricity on pontoons, stores in village half a mile away. Diesel can be brought from the village by truck: apply at the shop. A pleasant, quiet and friendly place. No dues in 1981.

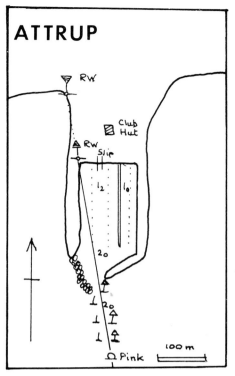

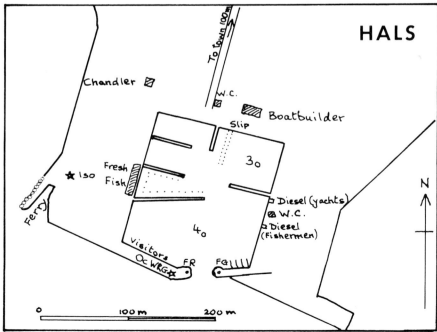

Aalborg
see chart 107

The two basins W of the bridge each have a pair of entrance buoys: yachts should berth in the Baadehavn (the more easterly basin) if room, otherwise in the Skudehavn. The port listens on Ch 16. There were still no dues in 1981, but they were under consideration. For bridge opening times see Passage Notes: Løgstør to Hals, above.

Aalborg is by far the largest town in the area and has all facilities. Sailmaker P. Mommsen at Borgergade 23 will carry out speedy repairs. There is a good chandler on the quay, and repairs to all types of hull except steel can be made. Diesel from pump near SW corner of Baadehavn: apply to Thomas Gede in small yellow house nearby. Chart agent in Borgergade beside sailmaker. All stores. Three yacht clubs and extra toilet buildings.

St Botolph's Cathedral dates from 1554, and the seventeenth century altarpiece and carved pulpit are worth seeing, as is the monastery of the Holy Ghost, still in use as a home for the old. The town also boasts a Tivoli amusement park, second only to that in Copenhagen.

Hals
see plan

An attractive old fortress town guarding the entrance to the Limfjord from the Baltic, with seventeenth century fortifications on which the cannon still look out over the sea. The entrance is straightforward: berth alongside the W outer wall, or as space allows.

There is a good chandler speaking good English (not common in this area) at Hals Marine Services, on the NW corner of the inner basin. He has good stocks of charts across to Sweden and as far S as N Sjaelland and Fyn. Good but insufficient loos and showers in the old boathouse, red brick in the middle of the north quay. Good fresh fish from the market on the W quay. Diesel from pump in NE corner of outer basin. Modest shops in the small town ¼ mile to the N. A pleasant place, but with little of special interest although the church dates from 1200. Dues Kr18 up to 10m, Kr30 over (1981).

Passage notes – Hals to Aarhus including Anholt

Many yachtsmen cut straight across to Anholt or at least to Gjerrild and Grenaa, which is a pity as they miss the beauties of the Mariager and Randers Fjords. The water is shoal 2 miles offshore near the entrance of these fjords so care is needed, but the entrances are well marked and present no difficulty though they would be dangerous in heavy onshore winds. Otherwise there is nothing in this area to worry a yacht of normal draft until the approaches to Aarhus, which lie between Helgenaes and the island of Samsø. The dangerous Mejlgrund (0.5m) lies in the middle of this passage, and as it is poorly marked it is best avoided by keeping well over to the steep-to Helgenaes side. At night the numerous sectored lights make navigating the area a simple matter.

Hals: the harbour is well protected in every sense!

A corner of Mariager

Øster-Hurup

Included for completeness, this artificial pier-end harbour 10 miles S of Hals cannot be recommended for the yachtsman. The bar in the entrance can have as little as 2m at ML, which is reduced to under 1½m in S to SE winds. The outer basin suffers from severe scend, and there is often little room in the inner one. Water at the inner end of the mole connecting the harbour to the shore (400m), and stores from the village, a good mile. A harbour for emergencies only! Dues (1981) Kr20.

Mariager Fjord

Perhaps the most beautiful fjord in Denmark (or equal top with Roskildefjord). If at all possible it should not be missed.

A yacht need only identify the inner of the two green conical buoys that mark the deep-water approach: from here the much smaller channel buoys are thickly strewn along both sides of the channel. There are also numerous pairs of leading beacons, the front one of the first pair being bright orange and visible for several miles. These transits, whose bearings are marked on chart 110 (necessary for intending visitors), can be useful for checking compass deviation, and if necessary constructing a whole new deviation card. Look out for currents, which can reach 2 knots and in the approach can run across the line of the channel.

Once through the entrance narrows two mooring buoys will be seen on the S side of the channel: these are maintained by the fjord yacht clubs and may be used by visitors. There is also a small jetty (2m) at Als Odde, but it is exposed to wash and swell, and the pilot launch takes up much of the space.

The channel is narrow and closely buoyed past Hadsund (lifting bridge, usual signals) to the cement factory N of Assens, after which the inner part of the fjord is deep apart from one or two spits, clearly charted. The upper fjord in particular is outstandingly beautiful, with rolling wooded hillsides and pastures, and cows with a passion for going into the water for a little paddle.

Hadsund

The main yacht harbour is W of the bridge, at the SE end of the town. There is only about 1.5m depth. Diesel alongside, chandlery and water. All stores in town. The town is not of much interest and most people will prefer to continue to Mariager. Harbour dues discretionary.

Mariager   *see inset on chart 110*

A new yacht harbour has been built E of the old harbour, so there is now plenty of room to visit this charming town. With normal draft it is safe to steer direct for the new pierhead once the boat has passed between the pair of entrance buoys: there is no need to keep to the leading line. In the harbour there is at least 2m, although the 1981 charts had still not been altered to show the results of dredging. Diesel available in cans only. Water and electricity on pontoons, otherwise little in the way of facilities.

The yacht club is open 24 hours during the season: it has a small loo and shower, and an 'honesty box' for (discretionary) harbour dues. The beautiful old town is one of my favourites in all Denmark and deserves thorough exploration: don't miss the fifteenth century abbey and its church, with interesting frescoes. Restaurants, including a magnificent and ancient *kro*, and all stores in town. I had an exceptional meal at the Landgangen Motel, along the coast road that runs NE from the harbour.

Hobro

At the head of Mariager Fjord. The yacht harbour was not shown on chart 110 as late as 1981, but it lies on the N side of the fjord ½ mile NE of the main commercial harbour, and the entrance has no hazards. The E wall and first jetty have 3m depth at the offshore ends to 2m inshore, the W jetties 2–1½m. Guests berth inside the small jetty at the SE corner: the yacht club ship lies to the outside of this jetty. Fuel, water, supplies from town, ½ mile. Dues discretionary (1981).

The passage up the fjord is very pretty, and the town has the remains of an eleventh century Viking camp or *Fyrkat* 2 miles to the SW, and a museum with Viking treasures and good silver and porcelain.

Randers Fjord

Coming from the N take care to avoid Boels Rev, with a 0.9m sounding more than a mile offshore, by passing outside the E cardinal buoy that marks its end. From the green conical offing buoy (Fl (3) G 10s) the channel is closely buoyed, and there are also transit markers. The whole fjord is shoal apart from the narrow dredged channel, which must never be left. The tide tends to counteract the current, so that the flood is slack while the ebb can reach 4 knots. The scenery is less beautiful than that in the Mariager Fjord but it has its own charm, rather like the wilder NE parts of the Norfolk Broads before the tourists came.

Setting eel nets, Randers Fjord

Udbyhøj Nord

see plan

This useful small harbour near the mouth of Randers Fjord has a tidal range of about 0.8m. The inside of the E pier is reserved for fishing boats, and the W corner is shoal, so visitors must berth at one of the jetties. The first of these has 1.9m and the inner one 1.7m, but remember that S winds can lower the water level by up to 0.7m: I had an awful job getting out once, and I only draw 1.2m. Tiny unisex loo and no other facilities, but nice *kro* (inn) in the village. Dues (1982) Kr20.

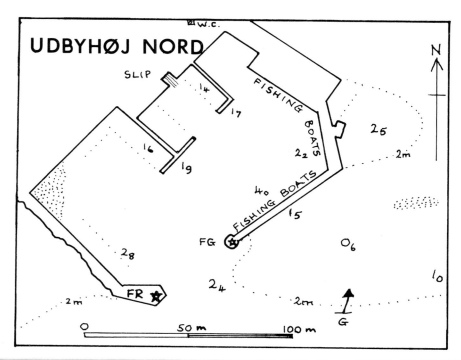

Udbyhøj Nord

Randers *see inset on chart 111*

The approach down the narrow buoyed channel is easy. There is a yacht harbour to starboard just before the town, but it is a long way from anywhere and there seems little reason to use it: to enter keep the two green posts close to starboard, when 1.4m will be found.

The main berth for visitors is in the Lystbaadehavn, in the N basin and marked on the chart inset. Water on quays. Metax, the filling station across the road from the NE corner of the yacht harbour, will deliver diesel alongside from a truck. The official minimum is 500 litres, to encourage yachts to club together, but the manager speaks good English and is disposed to be helpful to English yachts. Yacht club with loos; it is shut on Mondays, when the Roklub can be used. If no room, yachts may berth at the SW end of the N harbour. No harbour dues in 1981.

Randers is Denmark's sixth largest town, and has two sailmakers and excellent shopping: walk SW to the end of the N harbour and then turn right (NW) for main shopping area, about half a mile from the yacht harbour. The fifteenth century Helligaandhuset houses the Tourist Office and is worth a visit for its own sake, as is St Morten's church, circa 1500, which has a beautiful carved choir screen and pulpit.

Bønnerup *see plan*

This strategically important harbour lies some 4 miles W of the Gjerrild headland, and is a good jumping-off place for Anholt. Approaching from the W or NW, note that shoals extend a mile offshore both W and E of the harbour; also the Tangen shoal 5 miles NW of the entrance has a least charted depth of 2.3m, which could be reduced by more than $\frac{1}{2}$m at LW and with SE winds.

The main yacht jetty is in the E inner basin; berth there or as space allows. Loos and showers in the harbour office S of the E basin. The diesel pump is conveniently placed: for service try the Marineolie office in a hut on the S wall of the southernmost of the two W inner basins. Water on yacht jetty, shops in village, 200m. Dues were Kr25 in 1981, and collected at 0800 at that, which did not amuse my neighbour who had got in well after midnight, but this was cheap by standards further S, and the importance of the harbour justifies what locally was a rather high charge. Very much a staging point though: not pretty and nothing much to see, though there is a good bathing beach.

Anholt *see plan*

A charming and fascinating island, but sadly the harbour is usually painfully overcrowded in the holiday season, mainly July. The huge radar tower about 400m NE of the harbour entrance is a good landmark. Approach from the W is simple; only from the N and E must the long shoals that stretch out from the NW and NE points of the island be borne in mind.

The outer harbour is untenable owing to scend: yachts berth in the inner

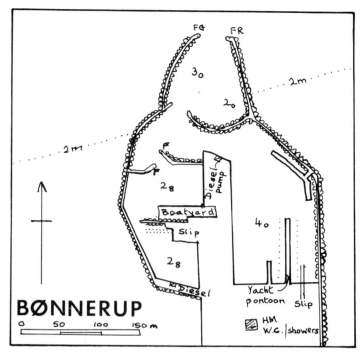

BØNNERUP

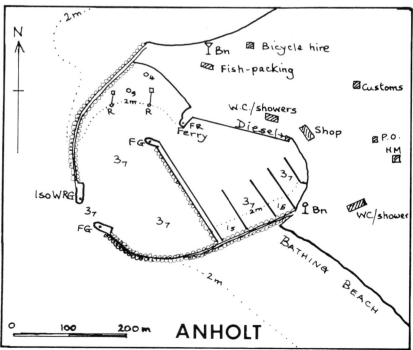

ANHOLT

harbour, bows to the breakwater or a jetty and stern to anchor. There is very little room to manoeuvre, and the stern anchor should be prepared and ready to let go before entering.

Water at the roots of the jetties, fuel from E end of ferry pier 9–10 a.m. only and not Sunday. Loos, showers and good shop in harbour, bicycle hire available and well worth it if you are not carrying your own. Dues among the highest in Denmark: Kr50 per day in 1981. However, if you arrive after 1800, the first two nights count as one.

The village is not much, but beyond it lies the Ørkenen, the desert, a marvellous area of dunes covered with junipers and other desert scrub and smelling wonderful. The coast SE from the harbour is a huge sandy beach, and once out of sight of the harbour bathing costumes become increasingly unfashionable.

Anholt is well worth a visit, but it is a shame that it has become *the* place for the climax of everyone's cruise, particularly for German yachtsmen, so if at all possible get there by mid-June or after the end of July.

Grenaa
see inset on chart 102

This major harbour, 30 miles SW of Anholt or 16 miles round the corner from Bønnerup, is the last on the way S before the shelter of the offshore islands begins and we reach the more fashionable cruising areas. Grenaa is a busy ferry port, and a good lookout is needed in the approaches.

Visitors berth along the N wall of the Sydhavn (though there was talk in

Anholt harbour, dominated by the radar tower

Anholt harbour

1981 of extending the yacht berths in the Nordhavn, at present for locals only). Diesel and water from the S side of the entrance to the Fiskerihavn. Sail repairs and chandlery from Gudmann & Son in Søgade, the westerly continuation of the N quay of the Fiskerihavn. Engine repairs available: ask at office (Havnkontor). Toilets (dirty, a rare event in Denmark) and showers 100m S of the Havnkontor: walk straight along N quay of Sydhavn and keep straight on. Shops in Strandgade, parallel to Søgade to the north; launderette in Kystvej, up Søgade and left over a small bridge; for the butcher turn right off Kystvej just before the launderette. Harbour listens on Ch 16, working Ch 12. Dues in 1981 Kr23 for 8–12m length: this covered two days. There is little of interest in the rather modern and industrial town.

Ebeltoft   *see plan*

A charming old town lying deep in a bay. Chart 112 covers it on the largest scale, but with the plan here chart 103 is quite adequate as long as the approach is made by daylight. Coming up the bay, the Sandhagen shoal is well marked by green conical buoys, after which a short buoyed channel leads to the harbours. The yacht harbour is the southernmost basin, the Skudehavn: berth there or in the Nordhavn if no room. Good loos and showers at the NE corner of the Skudehavn, water on pontoons. Exceptionally good chandler Baadshoppen on Vestvej between Skudehavn and Nordhavn. Diesel available alongside on request from Esso station on Sdre Strandvej, just inshore from the yacht harbour, 0800–1630. Dues Kr35 (1981).

The town is quite beautiful, with a particularly pretty *kro*. The old frigate *Jylland* used to lie in the Nordhavn, but there are plans to re-rig her and berth her outside the harbour as a museum ship. Ebeltoft is a place well worth the small detour involved by a visit.

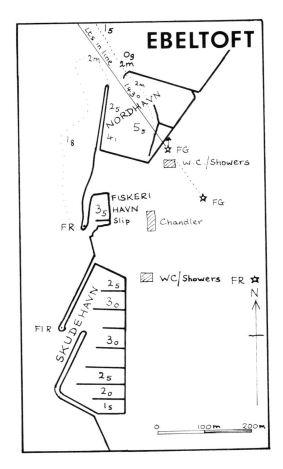

Nappedam

This nice little yacht harbour, built by local yachtsmen with their own hands, lies NNE of Aarhus in the Kalø Vig. Approach keeping about ½ mile off the E shore of the bight until the Ronsten beacon (Fl(3) R 10s) is seen, then leave it and a red buoy 300m NNE to port. From the buoy, a direct course can be steered for the harbour entrance. There is 3m along the outer walls; guests secure just to starboard of the entrance or as space allows.

Diesel from harbourmaster most of the day in season, water on jetties. Dues were Kr25–35 in 1981. Toilets are left open permanently, and the rest of the clubhouse may be used by visitors when open. No stores.

Egaa

An enormous marina that is the main yacht harbour for Aarhus, although it is a good 4 miles from the centre of that town. Approach from S of E, and enter through the gap *south* of the central mole: there is over 3m at the end of each of the eight pontoons, down to 2.2m near the roots. Super loos and

Ebeltoft

showers near the harbour office, fuel, all repairs, some stores and good bus service to Aarhus. Dues Kr35 (1981).

Aarhus   *see plan*
The yacht harbour is the northernmost of all the basins, with its own separate entrance. The approach has no hazards apart from the heavy traffic. The harbour is always very crowded, but the basin is 400m long and there is usually a hole somewhere if you look hard enough. Toilets at harbour office or yacht clubs. Aarhus Sejlklub is open 1000–2200, and does meals until 2100. Showers 0700–2200. The harbourmaster can hire bicycles, useful as the town centre is a good mile from the yacht harbour. Fuel from BP station open 1500–1900 weekdays, 0900–1600 Saturdays and Sundays. All repairs and facilities. Dues (1981) Kr30–40.

A Viking base and now Denmark's second city, Aarhus is rich in interest, and I can mention only a few of its features. Den Gamle By (The Old Town)

49

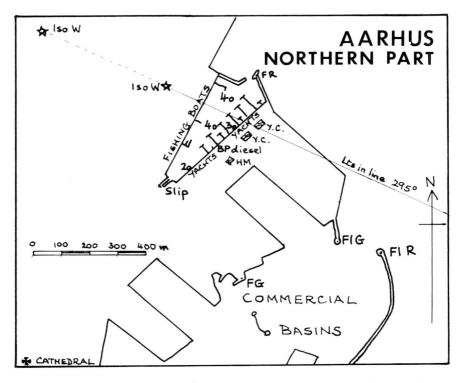

is an incredible collection of old houses, brought from all over Denmark and rebuilt, with collections of furniture, domestic equipment etc inside. The By can always be visited, and the collections are open every day from 10 to 5. The cathedral has a wonderful altarpiece by Bernt Notke, erected in 1479, and if time allows the Prehistoric Museum at Moesgaard (bus 6 from main railway station) has an extraordinary exhibit of an almost perfectly preserved man (one of the bog dwellers) from about the time of Christ, and outdoor reconstructions of buildings and houses from various periods.

II · From Kiel through the Lille Baelt (Little Belt) to Tunø and Norsminde

The Kiel Canal

The passage of this canal is dealt with briefly in my *Frisian Pilot*, but I should add that in recent years the entry signal of white over green lights is for commercial traffic only; yachts must wait for a single white light before entering a lock. The locks have floating pontoons at the sides (old tree-trunks, anyway!) and the water moves gently, so a passage of the canal is perfectly simple. If passing through without otherwise visiting Germany (and therefore uncleared by Customs) a boat should fly International Third Substitute, which avoids being boarded by Customs.

The Kieler Fjord

There are a great number of yacht harbours in the Kiel Fjord, as most German owners prefer to keep their boats in the Baltic rather than brave the hazards of the North Sea, and I would guess that around half of all German yachts are berthed in or around this fjord. I have therefore been selective in this area, and have omitted all the harbours in the fjord S of the canal entrance as most visitors will want to turn N for the open Baltic. However, there are good harbours at Mönkeberg, Düsternbrook and Wik.

Stickenhörn (British Kiel Yacht Club)   *see inset on chart 185*

The harbour lies about a mile NNE of the E entrance to the Kiel Canal. The Stickenhörn buoy (E cardinal, Q(3) 10s) is left to starboard and a course shaped between the land and the long mole projecting from the Friedrichsort shore.

The BKYC moorings are those at the extreme NW end of the inlet. Mooring is the usual stern to posts and bow to jetty, but the posts are very much heavier than normal so beware in case your carefully prepared bowlines are too small to go over the tops. The distance from posts to shore is also abnormally great in many cases, and boats arriving for the first time after being used to Danish harbours have been known to get into a terrible muddle.

The BKYC is a military unit of the British Army, and while they are very friendly and welcoming it must be remembered that they are on duty, not on

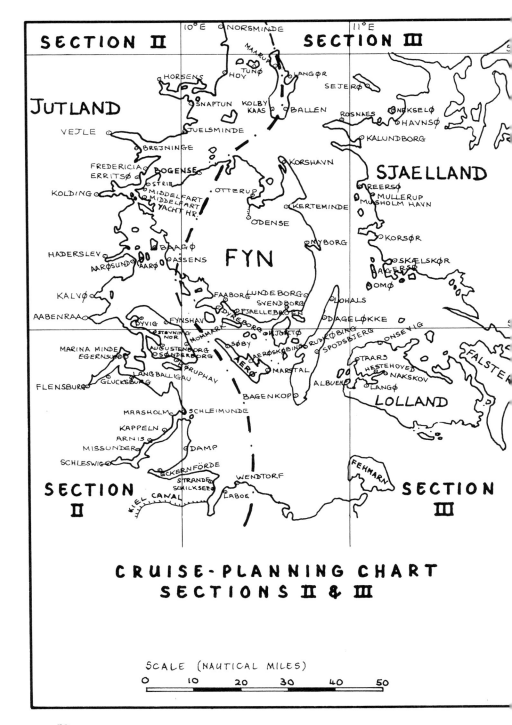

CRUISE-PLANNING CHART SECTIONS II & III

SCALE (NAUTICAL MILES)

holiday, and in particular that Army mechanics are not allowed to help out on civilian boats. Visitors are allowed to use the club, and also by a recent concession the NAAFI store. Dues (1981) DM10.

Laboe
see plan

This pleasant but crowded harbour is not marked on Danish chart 185 for some reason, but it lies on the E bank of the Kieler Fjord in latitude 54°24.1′N, just below a conspicuous windmill. Beware the line of posts with a beacon at each end SW of the entrance: they are virtually submerged at HWS. Water on jetties, fuel from tanker barge, loos and showers at yacht club as shown on plan. It is a jolly, crowded place with good shops nearby, but noisy and restless compared with the larger harbours further N. I must admit, though, that if I am in the mood for a convivial evening it is one of my favourites in the area.

Schilksee (Olympiahafen)

The larger and more southerly of the two yacht harbours shown on chart 185 in the Strander-Bugt. There is a N and a S basin, the former entered between the two main moles, the latter by passing S and W of the more southerly one.

This enormous harbour has usually plenty of visitors' berths, denoted by the usual Baltic red/green card system. No fuel is available (the fuelling berth at Strande, only half a mile away, serves both harbours) but there is a sailmaker, an excellent chandler, and the harbourmaster can arrange for repairs. 10 ton crane. All supplies from shops on the second floor of the huge

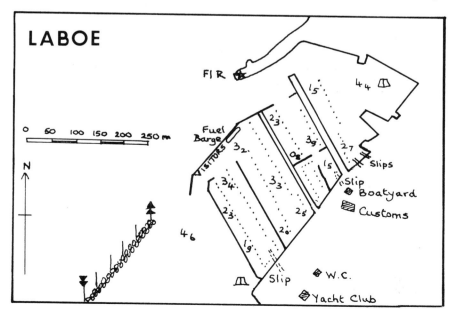

Laboe. The windmill on the skyline (centre) makes a good landmark.

Just part of the great Olympiahafen at Schiksee. Strande can be seen beyond.

building overlooking the harbour, sauna, swimming pool. Dues (1981) were based on quadratmeters (length × breadth in metres) and were DM11 for 15–30QM, DM17 30–40 etc. A strange place, its sheer size making it a little awesome and impersonal.

Strande
The more northerly of the two harbours in the Strander-Bugt and not so huge as Schilksee, though still large by normal standards. There is a small breakwater between the pierheads: it is possible to pass either side, but the E passage has much more water than the W one, which has about 2m. Berth as directed or where a green card shows. Fuel from the berth by the harbour office at the head of the central pier, toilets and showers at the root of the

same pier (key from HM, DM10 deposit). Sailmaker, repairs by arrangement through HM. Shops at NE corner of harbour, including a small supermarket with butcher and bakery. Yacht club, hotels and restaurants. Dues as for Schilksee. This is a pleasant harbour as commercial yacht harbours go, and a good place from which to begin a passage to Denmark.

Wendtorf   *see plan*
This harbour lies E of the entrance to the Kieler Fjord, and the entrance is rough and hard to find in strong N winds. The red offing buoy (Oc(2) R 9s) which lies a mile S of the westernmost of a group of four yellow buoys must be identified, when it can be approached from between N and W; at night there are also two FR leading lights on 148°. There are three pairs of channel buoys to the S, and then the channel bears round to the E, marked on both sides by port and starboard beacons. Perfect shelter in all weathers once inside.

Visitors can sometimes lie alongside before the first of the jetties, or find a free berth at one of them. Repairs at boatyard, loos and showers in harbour office building. No fuel. 28 ton Travellift. Club-restaurant, shops some distance away. Dues DM1 per metre (1981).

This is a nice, cheerful place, and like so many harbours with slightly tricky entrances, they are always pleased to see visitors.

Eckernförde
As it lies at the head of a wide and not especially pretty fjord, which incidentally has a torpedo range running along its S shore, there seems little

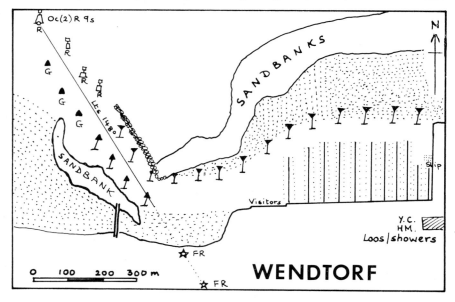

Wendtorf, a useful and friendly harbour E of the Kieler Fjord

reason for foreign yachts to visit this town, but it does have an excellent yacht harbour on the N shore, about a mile E of the town but W of the large naval harbour. The approach is straightforward; berth as space allows. Showers and loos ashore, water on pontoons, no really convenient shopping, though for keen cyclists or walkers the town is a pleasant holiday resort with good bathing to the S.

Damp

This unpromisingly named large harbour lies about 12 miles NW of the entrance to the Kieler Fjord, and can be a very useful staging point on the way N or S. The entrance is between two long piers, and guests moor inside the N one in the outer harbour, which can be a restless berth in E winds. Fuel, water on the jetties, loos and showers, Customs, supermarket, good bathing beach and a salt water swimming pool. A yachting and holiday development without any real town or places of interest nearby, but usefully placed some 3–4 hours from the Canal, and 4–5 hours from Sønderborg.

The Schlei

If you talk to German yachtsmen, you get the impression that there is nowhere in the whole of the German Baltic really worth visiting, and it is amazing how many of them know large areas of Denmark and yet have never visited the charming waters of their own Schleswig-Holstein, especially the Schlei and the Flensburg Fjord. I think both are well worth a visit, but I should point out that while I normally recommend Danish charts, German chart 41 is the only one to cover the Schlei, though Danish 154 is adequate for Flensburg Fjord. The scenery of the Schlei is very beautiful in good weather, the shores wooded with beech, willow and aspen. The blue, white and red horizontally striped flag seen everywhere in these waters is the standard of Schleswig-Holstein, not the Dutch ensign flown upside down.

Coming from the S, the enormous moles of Olpenitz naval harbour are a conspicuous mark: the entrance is a mile to the N. Coming from the N, the red and white radio tower a mile N of the entrance is conspicuous, and by my observations is 42m high, a useful figure which enables it to be used for distance off by sextant.

Navigation of the Schlei is straightforward as the channel is well buoyed; in many areas there is plenty of water for the average yacht well outside the channel. W winds produce an outgoing stream, which can reach 4 knots near the entrance, and also lower the water level. The pilot books say by up to 2m, but I think this must be very rare as it would mean losing over half the water in the entire fjord, but certainly in such conditions one should allow for perhaps 1m less depth than charted.

Schleimunde   *see plan on German chart 41*
This bleak little harbour cannot be recommended except for a boat on passage and in a hurry: its only advantage is in lying near the entrance. Boats lie bow to wall, stern to buoy. There is a small toilet, and limited stores are available.

Maasholm   *see plan on German chart 41*
Two miles up the Schlei from the entrance, this yacht harbour offers good comfort and convenient shopping. There are shops and banks close to the harbour, and the Yachtwerf Moderzitski can do repairs. Diesel is available in the Fischereihafen, and it is a pleasant though dull place to spend a night. Dues (1981) DM10 for 7–10m, DM12 10–15m.

Kappeln   *see inset on German chart 41*
There are long stretches of yacht berths both above and below the bridge, owned by various clubs and organisations, so all one can say is that there is usually a berth somewhere, which will have toilet and shower facilities of some sort. Opening signal for the bridge is two flags above each other in the shrouds and two long blasts on the horn, but it opens only on the hour and at that time there are usually enough boats waiting for the signals to be unnecessary. Diesel just above (S of) the bridge, on the E side. Once a member of the Hanseatic League, the town is old and charming, and has good shops but no special yachting facilities. There are boatyards above and below the bridge with slips up to 15 tons. Dues various, according to the ownership of the berth used.

Arnis   *see inset on German chart 41*
There is a full-scale marina, in a bay NW of the peninsula on which the village stands, approached by a 2m channel marked by green and red posts. There is usually plenty of room and it has showers, loos and all facilities. The village is a boatbuilding centre and has the yard of the major wooden builders Matthiessen & Paulsen. All repairs can be done, and there is a sailmaker. A nice little place, and worth a visit.

Lindau bridge over the Schlei

Missunde
see inset on German chart 41

There are several yacht jetties here and a yacht club. The best place for visitors is the Marina Brodersby, which operates the green card system. Stream can be strong after a change of wind. Restaurant, small shop, showers, loos etc. A very pretty little place, quiet and completely sheltered.

Schleswig
see inset on German chart 41

This beautiful and historic town lies at the head of the navigable part of the Schlei, and has two good yacht harbours. The Wiking yacht harbour is modern and shiny, with a skyscraper building (restaurant at the top, with marvellous views of the surrounding countryside) and all facilities. Dues are levied according to the size of 'box' occupied: a 10m box costs DM10, 12m DM12, or 15m DM15. Very good showers and loo at the S side of the harbour building, 8 ton crane, shops five minutes. Convenient for the Schloss Gottorf, but a long way from the main town.

Moorings in the old yacht harbour to the NE cost DM8 per night. There are loos and showers and two yacht clubs of which the best is the Schlei S.C., open every day except Tuesday and light meals available. For engine repairs enquire at the club.

The Cathedral of St Peter (Domkirke) simply must not be missed: among its many treasures are a painted woodcarving of the three kings from about 1300, a wonderful Renaissance marble of Friedrich I (1552), and above all the early sixteenth century Brüggemann altar on which the carvings depict the entire New Testament story. The Schloss Gottorf should also be visited, both for the building itself and for the museums, which include in their collections the beautiful Cranach 'Adam and Eve', and some fascinating finds from peat bogs ranging from statues (Iron Age man obviously went in for bottoms rather than bosoms!) to large fourth century ships. But apart from the obvious tourist places, Schleswig is a charming town to wander in, especially the old town south of the cathedral. For the cruising man with time to spare, the whole expedition up the Schlei (Schleimunde to Schleswig is about 25 miles) and back can be a highly attractive way of spending two or three days.

Flensburg Fjord

This fjord, spelt **Flensborg** by the Danes, has some pleasant harbours both on the German and on the Danish sides, the frontier running down the middle. The upper shores of the fjord are heavily wooded, and it is a pleasant cruising area. The entrance is partly closed off by the Kalkgrund shoal, which projects N from the Birk headland and is marked at its N end by a light tower. The stream can be strong N of this shoal, and shallow–draft boats can cut across the shoal in 2.5m at normal level by keeping No.5 buoy in line with the yellow buoy (Fl(2) Y 9s) a mile N of the point of the headland. There is a special chart (154) for the fjord, but Danish 152 is perfectly adequate. There are shoals in the narrows around Holnis, S of Egernsund, but these are clearly charted and well buoyed, and present no problem as long as care if taken.

Langballigau   *see plan*

A cheerful, noisy holiday resort on the S (German) side of the Flensburg Fjord, among heavily wooded hills. The approach has no hazards, and as most of the moorings are alongside there always seems to be room for one more boat, even though the harbour gets very full at weekends. There are 300 berths, of which 60 are for guests. The SE part of the harbour is shoal.

Schleswig

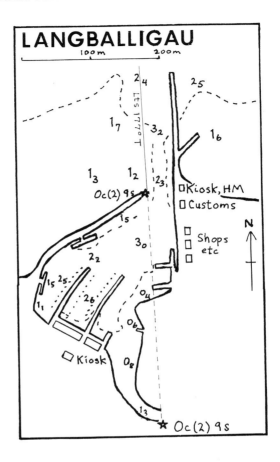

Stores from very de luxe kiosk at the E side of the harbour mouth, where the harbourmaster's building, with good loos and showers, is also to be found. Several restaurants, and a proper shop about 200m S of the harbour. Duty-free stores are available from the kiosks on the E side of the harbour: they are very cheap (£1 for a litre of brandy in 1981) but must be ordered one day ahead. Dues DM7.90 for 8–10m, DM11.30 10–12m. 'Over that size you are too big for my harbour' the HM said!

Marina Minde, Egernsund

A new artificial harbour lying on the N (Danish) shore of the Flensburg Fjord, about a mile SE of the town of Egernsund. It has 220 berths and there always seems to be plenty of room. It is clearly marked on chart 152, and there is no need for a plan as it is a square harbour with 2–3m on every jetty.

The harbourmaster is helpful and speaks good English. There is a good food shop, a kiosk and a bar at the harbour. The town is 15 minutes' walk; nothing of great interest but all stores. First-class loos and showers, water

Cheerful chaos in Langballigau

and electricity on jetties. Good bathing beaches on the way to town.

For repairs or the yacht club it is necessary to go into the town harbour through the swing bridge, or the harbourmaster will phone for a mechanic. (He also supplied me, when I arrived there singlehanded, with a nice light small boy who cheerfully allowed himself to be hoisted to the masthead to recover a burgee that had got jammed under the forestay and pulled off its staff.) Bicycles and ponies for hire. Dues (1981) Kr30 up to 10m, Kr45 10–13m, Kr60 over.

Glücksburg

see plan

Headquarters of the Flensburg Yacht Club and one of the most beautiful yacht harbours I have ever visited, with beech forest coming right down to the ends of the pontoons.

The harbour is not clearly shown on chart 152, but lies just E of the N cardinal buoy Glycksburg N. Visitors are most likely to find a berth on the W pontoon, which involves quite a long walk to the club, but it is so pretty that no one is likely to mind as long as it isn't raining. The pontoon is kept locked: key (DM20 deposit) from harbour office. There is a loo on this pontoon (not recommended), and excellent loos and showers (free) at the beautiful club. This is open every day and serves good food, but lunch must be ordered first thing in the morning, and supper by lunchtime. The nearest

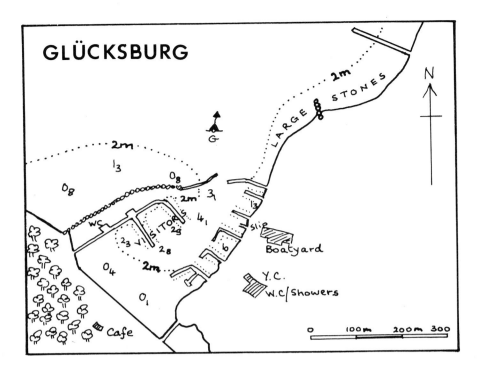

Flensburg. This is the naval yacht harbour, and may not be used.

shop is 20 minutes' walk, but there is a cafe overlooking the harbour. Splendid walks through the beech woods beside the fjord.

Flensburg

A large, impressive town, but the best yacht berths are a fair distance from the centre.

Approaching, the large yacht harbour on the E side of the fjord below the palace and just N of the naval jetties must be ignored: it is for naval personnel and their visitors only. S of the naval moorings there is a straight-sided basin about 400m long, cut into the E shore. This is the best place for visitors; it is the harbour of Flensburger Yacht Service and is quiet and sheltered, unlike the few berths in the main commercial harbour which are disturbed by constant wash.

Boats lie to jetty and buoy. Water on pontoons, fuel barge, toilets at the top of the harbour, and FYS provide chandlery, repairs, charts etc and have a 12 ton crane. Sailmaker and all stores in town, but the centre is a good mile from the berths.

Passage notes – Kieler Fjord to Tunø by the Little Belt

As far as the entrance to the Flensburg Fjord, there is nothing to be added to what has been said above. From here, there is a choice of proceeding N by the Little Belt proper, or by Sønderborg, the Alssund and the Alsfjord. The main Little Belt route has two dangerous shoals near the N end of Als, about $2\frac{1}{2}$ miles offshore, and shoals run offshore from the Als coast in several places. However, all are well marked and present no real problems to the careful navigator. (The waters E of Skjoldnaes, the NW point of Aerø, will be dealt with in Section III.) N of Als the waters widen and then narrow; Aarø in particular is shoal, especially on its NE side, but there are well marked channels W of Aarø and both W and E of Baagø. N of here there are no navigational problems until N of Trelde Naes, but it is worth remembering that the current can be strong in the narrows S of Fredericia, southgoing in strong N or W winds and northgoing in strong S or E winds, up to 2 knots.

The waters W of Samsø require special care, owing to numerous shoals. The easiest route is to cut over to the SW corner of Samsø and keep close in to its W coast, which is clean except for a bank extending W from Ringebjerge, but there is the buoyed Søgrund passage NW of Endelave with a least depth of 3m at ML: this can be tricky to find in poor visibility. N of here the going is clear to Tunø, but note that Tunø Knob, to its W, is not only shoal but also a wildlife sanctuary which should not be approached.

Høruphav   *see plan*

This harbour lies slightly out of the way, in a blind fjord 4 miles E of Sønderborg, but it is a pleasant little place. The water is shoal 400m offshore S of the entrance, so it is important not to steer for the entrance until it bears

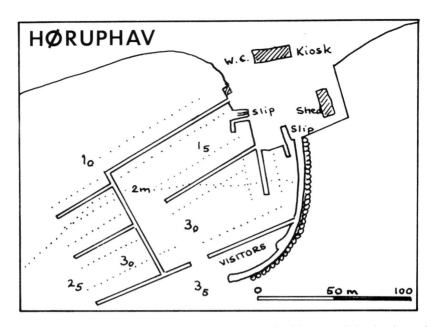

W of N. Berth as space allows, but note that the N part of the harbour is shoal both inside and out.

There is water on the jetties, and the kiosk has limited food. Good loos and shower beside kiosk, and there is a fair sized hotel. Dues (1981) Kr25 up to 8m, Kr30 8–12m. Fuller supplies, bank etc in village, $\frac{1}{2}$ mile.

Sønderborg
see plan

The new yacht harbour lies at the S end of the town, but most visitors continue to use the old harbour where one may lie alongside the quays on the E side of the sound, S of the bridge being more comfortable and convenient. Look out for current up to $2\frac{1}{2}$ knots when mooring. Dues were Kr20 up to 10m, Kr30 over in 1981, while the yacht harbour charged Kr22 and 34. The excellent shops of the town are only three minutes' walk from the quays.

The bridge (usual signals) does *not* open between the following times: Mon–Fri 0629–0700, 0730–0800, 0813–0828, 0913–0928, 1100–1115, 1124–1139, 1200–1215, 1300–1328, 1502–1530, 1600–1700, 1729–1745, 1955–2010. On Fridays only it is also closed 1815–1845 and 1915–1945. Saturday closures are 0629–0644, 0813–0828, 0913–0928, 1015–1030, 1115–1139, 1145–1200, 1313–1328, 1502–1517, 1745–1800, 1917–1932; and Sundays 0813–0828, 1124–1139, 1313–1328, 1502–1517, 1729–1744, 1914–1929, 1955–2010, 2307–2322. In general, the bridge opens just before and just after each closed period, and is rather reluctant to open at other times except during fairly long open periods, or when there is very little road traffic.

Sønderborg harbour is dominated by the castle which is well worth a

Sønderborg: the Christian X bridge is open

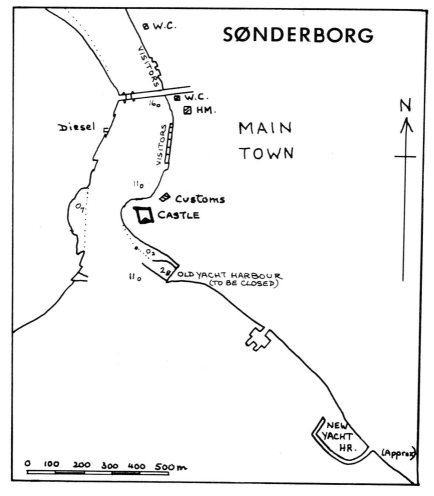

visit, Queen Dorothea's Chapel having some nice pieces. The Dybbøl Mill a mile W of the bridge is also worth visiting if you are feeling energetic. It was at a battle here that Denmark lost South Slesvig until it was returned after the First World War. The mill is open 10–6 during July and 1–4 pm during the rest of the summer season.

Augustenborg
see plan

A pleasant small town with a beautiful eighteenth century castle and lying at the head of a short fjord, Augustenborg is a particularly good place to leave a boat for the winter.

Navigation of the fjord presents no problems and the narrow channel near the head is plentifully buoyed. The moorings on the N side are owned by the town, cost Kr25 per night (1981), and have poor public loos, water on the pontoons and nothing else. The marina on the S side has plenty of room, costs more (Kr35 for 6–9m, Kr40 9–11m in 1981), but has good toilets and showers and a nice *kro*. Water and electricity on the jetties. Diesel can be got from the filling station on the N side of the dam across the fjord; they have wheeled tanks holding 100 litres which can be pushed down to the yacht harbour and from which a boat can be refuelled alongside. The marina has masses of space where boats can be left in the open or under cover, and a permanent winter staff.

The town has really good shops and a nice old hotel. The royal castle is now mostly a sanatorium for nervous diseases, but the Queen uses it occasionally during the summer. It has a most beautiful chapel, decorated in typical eighteenth century style in blue and gold. The key can be borrowed from the porter in the office marked Information in a side building on the N side of the castle. A very quiet, restful spot.

Augustenborg Palace

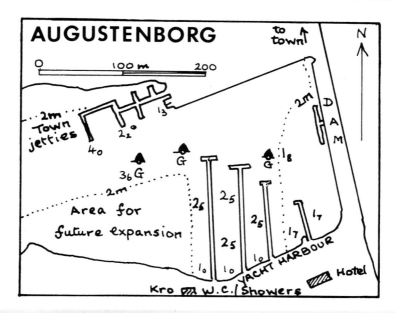

Augustenborg: the town moorings are on the left, the marina on the right.

Stevning Nor

A small bay at the mouth of Augustenborg Fjord that is exposed to W winds, and should not be used when winds from SW to W over force 5 are expected, but it is an idyllic spot for a picnic or an overnight stop in settled weather. The yacht jetty is the one on the N side of the inlet and has over 2m at the end; the one on the S side is too shallow for anything but motor cruisers. No facilities, not even water or loos.

67

Dyvig

see plan

This lagoon at the N end of the Als Fjord offers a charming and unusual place to spend a night, either on a jetty or at anchor. The approach is via Stegsvig; as the plan shows the narrows are well buoyed so chart 152 is quite adequate for the entrance. Mooring at the *kro* jetty is bow to wall, stern to anchor; the moorings to the E and S have posts. Dues vary around Kr25 (1981), nothing for lying at anchor. I found plenty of room at 1700 on a Wednesday afternoon in July, the high season, but every berth was filled within half an hour and at weekends it would be wise to arrive by 1600 to ensure a berth. There is a kiosk by the *kro*, and toilets, water tap and clubhouse at the E side.

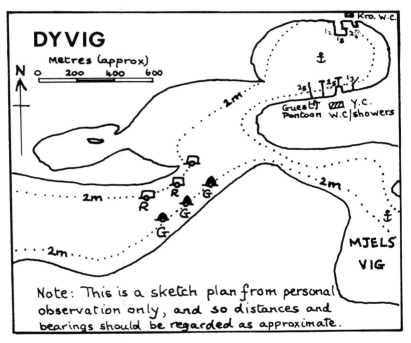

Aabenraa

see plan

The pleasant town lies at the head of a short fjord and has a good yacht harbour just S of the large commercial harbour. Yachts may also berth in the northernmost basin (Nyhavn), but as the moorings are on the E side of the basin the distance to the town centre is nearly as great, and the surroundings are industrial and dirty, so the yacht harbour should be used if at all possible.

Dues should be paid voluntarily at the club: except for late arrivals an extra charge is levied if they are not paid by 2000. There are several notices warning of this practice, but not in English. They were Kr30 up to 10m, Kr40 over in 1981. Fuel pontoon (apply to club for service), good

Narrows at the entrance to Dyvig. I am following an American yacht in.

A corner of Aabenraa

supermarket nearby. The club serves food 12–2 and 5–9. Water on jetties, good showers and loos.

The museum at 33 H.P. Hanssensgade is worth a visit for its collection of ships in bottles, and do not miss St Nicolaj's church, thirteenth century with a lovely baroque altarpiece from 1642 and a splendid carved pulpit.

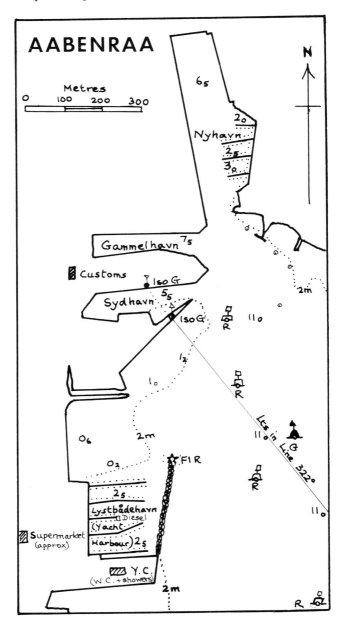

Mommark
see plan

This pleasant harbour on the E coast of Als is available for those taking the main Little Belt passage rather than the prettier and more sheltered route through the Als Fjord. It is most uncomfortable in winds with a northern component, but a new mole was planned in 1981 which when built should cure this fault. There is a good shop whose owner is also the harbourmaster, and speaks good English. Loos and showers beyond the *kro*, which is reputedly good and certainly expensive. Diesel alongside from small tank. Dues (1981) Kr30 per boat.

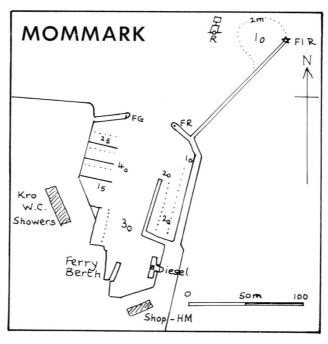

Fynshav
see plan

I have never visited this harbour, as the conditions were unsuitable when I was in the neighbourhood, but it was reputed to be very attractive. However, it was destroyed by gales in the winter of 1981–2, and not rebuilt by the following summer. Readers must therefore make local enquiries as to whether the harbour has been reinstated before attempting a visit.

Kalvø
see plan

A very tiny harbour with few facilities, but in a beautiful situation. There is not much water, the best being outside the harbour proper in a position exposed to the E: in W winds the water level can fall by well over a metre, leaving much of the basin dry.

There is a water tap with hose, and small clean loos but no showers. A hotel is open 10 a.m. to 11 p.m., serving meals 12–2 and 5–9. Stores only from Genner, over a mile. Dues (1981) Kr20 up to 10m, Kr30 over. A pleasant place to spend a night in good weather.

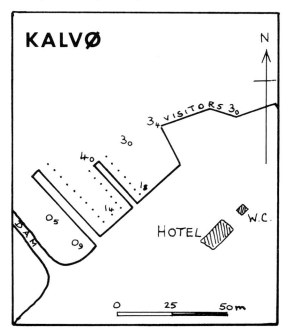

Kalvø harbour. A tiny harbour but beautifully situated.

Aarø

The harbour is clearly shown on chart 151, in the bay N of the lighthouse, and there seems no need for a plan as it is plain and square, with 2m depth all over the outer basin, and 2½m in the inner one. Like its neighbour Aarøsund it is often overcrowded, and if there is no room one may have to cross the sound to Assens. Water and showers, no fuel. Shops 500m away include a baker; there is a *kro* in the village serving meals 12–2 and 5–8. Dues Kr30 in 1982. A popular place for weekenders from some of the bigger towns nearby, but I am not enthusiastic.

Aarøsund   *see plan*

This little harbour has a very narrow and tricky entrance, and tends to be grossly overcrowded. Visitors normally have to moor across the ends of occupied slots, and climb ashore over other boats. No water, but loos, showers and small shop. Dues (1981) Kr20. I enjoyed squeezing in, but did not think it worthwhile to stay: I hate having to turn out at 5 a.m. because the owner of one of the slots inside wants to go for a sail!

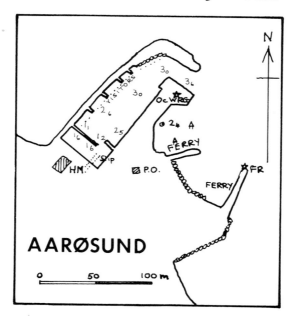

Assens   *see inset chart 151*

This large yacht harbour on the E side of the Little Belt lies in the same latitude as Aarø, but is a much safer bet for staying a night as there is always room. Berth as space allows. Water on jetties, diesel on pier D (ring bell for service), nice loos and showers open 24 hours, though there are not really enough of them so there are often long queues in the mornings. 15 ton Travellift. Club, cheapish restaurant. All repairs except to sails from Assens

Baatcenter. Small provision shop in the harbour, and tiny launderette in toilet building.

Dues in 1981 were rather high for the area: Kr40 for 7–12m, Kr50 over. The town is nearly a mile away and not of great interest, though there are some nice old buildings here and there and the Late Gothic Church of Our Lady, completed in 1488, merits a visit.

Assens yacht harbour

Haderslev Fjord

There is a special chart, Danish 153, covering this fjord, but I have to confess that I have never seen it, and for a yacht I would say it is quite unnecessary as the tricky entrance is well shown on chart 151 and the narrow channel leading from there to Haderslev is well marked. There is a small yacht jetty near the mouth of the fjord, just W of Stagodde on the S bank, which has about 1½m depth, perhaps more at the offshore end. This would be a possible stopping place for a night if in too much of a hurry to make the trip up to Haderslev. The buoyed channel carries 6m all the way up to Haderslev. While not as beautiful as the Mariager or Roskilde Fjords, this is a pretty fjord and well worth the detour.

Haderslev

There is no need for a plan as the harbour is simply the inner end of the fjord. Yachts moor on both sides. There is an inner basin on the S side about 200m before the bridge; it is difficult to identify as boats moor outside as well as inside. Water on the jetties. There are two yacht clubs on the S bank: toilets open 24 hours and shower in HSF motorboat club. Diesel, oddly enough, from HSC, the sailing club, but it is not open every day. Fibreglass repairs can be done at Ib.H. Neilsen's Baadevaerft, on the S bank E of the harbour area. There is a launderette at the S side of the bridge at the end of the harbour, and a large supermarket at its N end.

The town is full of beautifully restored old buildings, with very fine eighteenth century ones as well as the more frequently seen half-timbered style. The Cathedral of Our Lady, a Gothic brick church of the thirteenth and fourteenth century, should also be seen. It has a good carved pulpit from 1636, and the highest nave in all Scandinavia, the vaulting rising to 72ft above the floor.

Baagø

The harbour lies near the SW corner of the island, 2 cables NE of the lighthouse, and is formed by a simple L-shaped pier. The basin has 3m in its E half, and $2\frac{1}{2}$ at the W side. Slot berths, moor where green card shows, often crowded. There are water taps on the quay and dubious toilets and showers. A few simple stores are available at the harbour kiosk, otherwise one must go to the little town in the middle of the island, a good mile but a pretty walk. The old smithy in the village is worth seeing, and the N part of the island is wild and marshy with many interesting birds. Good bathing beaches near the harbour.

Middelfart Lystbaadehavn (Yachtharbour)

This harbour, known in the German pilot as **Russelbaek**, lies in a bay in the Faenø Sound S of the town of Middelfart. It is clearly shown on chart 151, except for a post with orange ball top to be left to port on entering. There is 3m on every jetty, and in 1981 it was newly finished and still relatively empty; in any case it is very big, so there should always be a berth free somewhere for visitors.

In 1981 there was water on the jetties, a snack bar, loos and showers, harbour office but little else; however, there were plans for a clubhouse, cafeteria and fuel berth. Bread can be ordered at the snack bar for collection next morning and they sell milk, otherwise stores in the town $\frac{3}{4}$ mile away.

Kolding Fjord

As with Haderslev Fjord, there is a special chart (156), which is hardly necessary for a yacht bound up the fjord as the channel is well marked, and in any case there is more than 2m depth everywhere except close inshore. But note that W winds can lower the water level by up to $1\frac{1}{2}$m. There are several yacht jetties along the shores of the fjord.

Kolding

Approaching the town, a large yacht harbour will be seen on the S bank as

Under autopilot, single-handing up Kolding Fjord

clearly shown on chart 151, but I would recommend a visitor to continue in the buoyed channel through the main harbour entrance and turn N once inside, into the old yacht harbour which is more conveniently placed and generally has room. There is a short pier equipped with finger berths on one side, below the clubhouse just W of the main yacht harbour, and this is the best bet for visitors, either on the fingers or alongside the other side.

There is an automatic fuel pump which takes Kr20 notes, water and electricity on the jetties, and good showers and loos 50m from the recommended berth. The yacht club is large, prosperous and friendly and has an excellent restaurant. There is a good chandler (open Sundays 10–2) with a small food section, and a sailmaker, Fusseng in Sønderhavnegade. Baae–Marin, near the club, can carry out motor and hull repairs. Their crane is only 7 tons but cranes up to 56 tons are available in the commercial harbour. All stores in the town, $\frac{3}{4}$ mile. The thirteenth century Koldinghus, partly destroyed by fire in 1808, is worth seeing, and do not miss Helligkorsgade which has magnificent old houses.

Kolding is only an hour by train from Esbjerg, which makes it an ideal spot for changing crews, and it would also be an excellent choice for leaving a boat for a week or two, or even over the winter.

Middelfart Gamlehavn (Old Harbour)

This harbour lies on the N side of Middelfart town, and it can only be recommended for a shopping stop now that the yacht harbour has been built. The basin is wide open to the surprisingly heavy swell and wash and is highly uncomfortable, but it is much closer to the shops and to the old part of the town, which is most attractive. There is also a little yacht harbour at Kongebro, only suitable for boats up to an absolute maximum of 9m length overall. This is just E of the bridge W of the town: beware a false entrance at the SE end of the little harbour, which is shoal and does not lead in. The real entrance is NW of the harbour. Dues rather high (Kr40 for 7–10m in 1981) and no facilities beyond rather primitive loos.

Streams in the Middelfart Narrows

The streams can run strongly between Fredericia to the N and the S end of Faenø to the S, and it is worth knowing that useful eddies can usually be found.

With a *north-going* stream, a south-going eddy will be found close inshore from just off Erritsø yacht harbour down to the bridge W of Middelfart; another runs along the other shore close in from off Middelfart Old Harbour round to Faenø and down the W side of that island. Note that there are four pillars to the old bridge W of Middelfart, numbered from the S. Eastbound vessels are required to pass between pillars 1 and 2, westbound between 3 and 4.

With a *south-going* stream, north-going eddies occur close in to the N shore of Faenø (using the Faenø Sound), close in round the headland W of Middelfart as far as the W bridge, and inshore from the E end of Middelfart all the way out of the narrows, except for the N side of the Strib peninsula. This is the easier run to make against a foul current as it does not involve crossing to the wrong side of a main channel.

Middelfart Bridge

Strib
see plan

There are two basins at Strib, the one for yachts being the more southerly. The entrance is very narrow, but a 30ft boat can just manoeuvre once inside. Berth at a free space, or alongside the NE wall near the end of the harbour. This harbour seems to be little used by visitors and is a useful alternative if Erritsø is full. Water, loos and showers. Dues (1981) Kr25. Stores from the village, ½ mile away. Good bathing beach near the lighthouse; for good swimmers only because of strong currents and eddies.

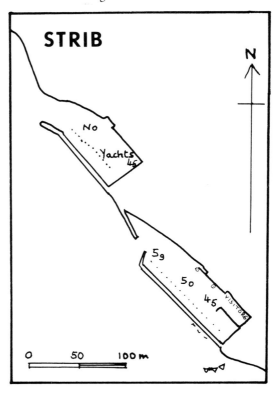

Erritsø Yacht Harbour
see plan

Now the main yacht harbour for the large town of Fredericia, although yachts are also allowed to lie in two of the basins of the commerical harbour there (see next entry).

Erritsø tends to be severely overcrowded and it is wise to get there by 1630 to be sure of a berth. After hours, latecomers can moor alongside the fuel quay but have to move first thing in the morning. There are two yacht clubs with restaurants (the motorboat club I know to be good – the other may well be, too) and a chandler with a small food section. A grocer will be found 200m S of the harbour. Fuel from the fuel quay, electricity and water on the jetties. Toilets and showers are good, but long queues in the morning.

Fredericia is 1¼ miles away. Fredericia harbour is not much closer to the station, so Erritsø is a good place for changing crews as the station is on the main Esbjerg line.

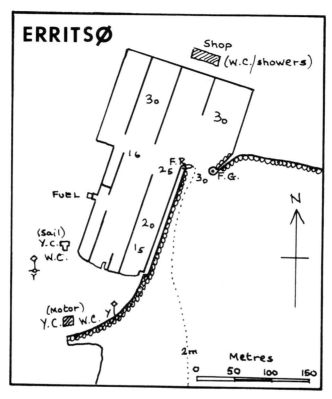

Fredericia
see inset on chart 151

Yachts are allowed to lie inside the W breakwater of the W basin (Vesthavn) or, in great noise and often chemical fumes, at the top end of the old harbour (Gamlehavn). The latter berth is close to the shops, and might make a useful day stop for a spree in the town, but I would choose the W basin for a night stop if I had to stay there at all. Note that the stream across the harbour entrance is always easterly, regardless of the direction of the current in the Little Belt.

Bogense
see inset on chart 114

This quiet port on the N coast of the island of Fyn falls naturally into this section: the Odense Fjord, 16 miles farther E, is on the borderline and I have covered it in the next section.

The main approach to Bogense is from the N and carries 4.2m depth, but there is a buoyed channel from the W with over 2m which is safe for most yachts in good weather and visibility. Once in, one can berth in the modern marina on the starboard hand, or keep to port and enter the old harbour which is nearer the shops but has no facilities. The chart shows two mid-channel soundings of 0.9m: these have no basis as far as I can determine (and would, of course, make the harbour unusable). The marina has all facilities including fuel and good loos and showers: the harbourmaster is helpful and speaks good English. There is a grocer/chandler at the SE corner of the yacht harbour and a bigger chandler, capable of all repairs, on the NE side and near the end of the old harbour. In 1981 the harbour offered free slipping and the very cheap use of a crane. Dues Kr40 (1981). We are back in the area of perceptible tides here, and Bogense has a mean rise and fall of 0.5m. The old town is very pretty, with Østergade offering some of the best buildings, and there is a copy of the famous Brussels Manneken Pis statue opposite the tourist office in Adelgade 26.

Vejle Fjord

There is a special chart for this fjord, but it is perfectly well covered by chart 114. There are one or two short spits off headlands, but all are plainly marked, as is the final channel through the shallows near the head of the fjord. In NW winds over force 5 there is some funnelling, and the water can be surprisingly rough until past Holtserhage.

Vejle

Entering the harbour, the yacht basin will be seen immediately on the N side: yachts should berth here. Only if there is no room or with very large yachts should one berth at the W end of the commercial harbour, in which case the boat must not be left unattended until the harbourmaster has been contacted and a berth agreed.

Traeskohage light, Vejle Fjord

The yacht harbour has a nice club open 0900–2200, restaurant closed Wednesdays. There is a sailmaker, Rasmussen in Toldbodvej, and Børresens near the yacht harbour can do repairs. There is a good chandler at the W end of the harbour, and the UnoX station there will supply diesel by truck. Water on the jetties. Dues (1981) Kr20. The town is about $\frac{3}{4}$ mile away: the walk is across some pretty rough country, so mind your ankles (also on the jetties in the yacht harbour itself, but they may well have been renewed by now).

The town is of considerable size, being the commercial and shopping centre for East Jutland, and has many points of interest. St Nicolai Church in Kirkegade has a rare altarpiece from 1791, later than most of those in Denmark, and a carved Renaissance pulpit. The Town Hall is also worth seeing, not for itself but for the old clock from a monastery that previously occupied the side.

Brejninge

This charmingly set yacht harbour lies on the S shore of the Vejle Fjord about 6 miles from Treldenaes, and has 2m depth. Dues in 1981 were Kr25, and there were primitive loos and showers, no fuel. Stores from the village, nealy a mile.

Juelsminde

see plan

A cheerful and friendly little harbour lying in a bay that is wide open to the E: the approach can be rough in strong E winds but once inside the shelter is good. Visitors berth alongside on the inside of the E pier. Water from tap and hose. There is a diesel pump at the base of the pier, and a particularly good fish shop on the SE quay. The excellent yacht club has loos and showers, open 0700–2200, and does good meals. There is a boatbuilder on the W wall. Shops in town, ten minutes' walk, include a chandler, Visø Marine, in the main street. Dues in 1981 were Kr35 for 9–12m, Kr40 over. Good bathing near the harbour.

Kolby Kaas

The harbour is on the SW coast of Samsø, and is shown clearly on chart 114. The approach is straightforward, and yachts moor in the S basin, in a vacant slot or alongside the inside of the S pier. This is very much a ferry port and has few facilities: there are poor toilets and showers and a shop, open 0700–2100 every day, 600m up the hill along the one road. Water hose on the middle of the W wall. Uncomfortable in NW winds. Not recommended except to break a passage.

Horsens Fjord

The only safe approach to this interesting and unusual fjord is through the narrow sound between Hjarnø and the mainland: this is well marked and presents no problems, although the current can run hard. There is a useful

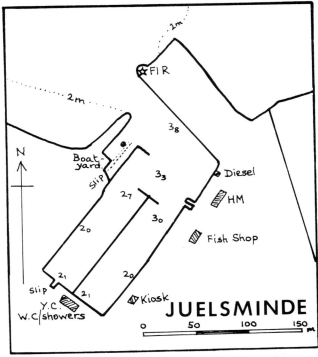

little harbour, Snaptun, in this sound, otherwise the only port is Horsens itself, although beautiful sheltered anchorage can be found (sounding in with care) N of Alrø. In spite of having blown a mainsail to pieces in these waters, it is one of my favourite areas in the less well known parts of the SW Baltic. The special chart (113) is unnecessary.

Snaptun

This little harbour opposite Hjarnø hardly merits a plan as it is almost perfectly square. The ferry presents no problem, as it lies outside the N pier; visitors lie alongside on the inside of the same pier, or in a vacant slot on the S side if room. There is at least 2.5m everywhere in the basin except in the S corner near the slip. Poor loos near the root of the N pier. Diesel from pump: apply to Hoki (the main shop) for service.

This is a useful place for stocking up on passage, with two shops and a hotel as well as fuel and water (hoses on the E pier: go alongside a fisherman if necessary while filling).

Horsens

The new yacht harbour is the first entrance on the N side just before the main harbour entrance: there is usually room. Exceptionally, the green card system was not in use in 1981. There is 2m throughout this basin. Alternatively, the first entrance to starboard inside the main harbour moles is another smaller yacht harbour: it has only 1.8m. Berth as space allows. S to SW gales can lower the water level by up to a metre.

Water is on the jetties, diesel from an automatic dispenser taking Kr20 notes on the W wall of the Fiskerihavn, the basin immediately W of the old (inner) yacht harbour. The nice yacht club has good loos and showers, and also a restaurant: when it is shut another lot are available beyond the clubhouse. There is an excellent sailmaker Anker Jepsen (ask at the club) and a small chandler with a few local charts.

The town centre is a good mile away but all stores are available there. Visitors should not miss the abbey church, built about 1200, with its rich woodcarvings; there are also a number of beautiful old houses, especially in Søndergade.

Hov

This small harbour is usefully placed for yachts, and the ferries have now been moved to a new harbour to the NE. When I visited it in 1981, however, it was best avoided except in emergency as it was crowded with fishing boats, restless with ferry traffic, and noisy and dirty. If entering, note that the whole of the W wall is shoal close in, so yachts can lie only on the E wall, or on the N side of the jetty formerly used for ferries.

Maarup   *see plan*

A tiny harbour on the W coast of Samsø and one of my favourites: in fact I prefer it to the area's best-known beauty spot, Tunø. The approach channel is buoyed, and yachts may berth in either basin but not alongside either side of the central pier. A kiosk open 0800–2100 sells simple stores and collects

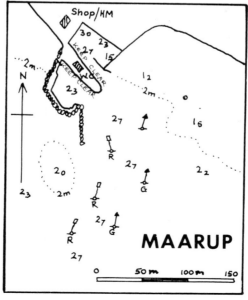

dues: Kr30 up to 10m in 1981, over that Kr40 but you would have a job to get in anyway! Good loos and showers in building on the central pier, stores in the village 1 mile away.

Tunø

A small and usually overcrowded harbour on the E side of the charming little island. Tunø has the unusual feature of having its lighthouse mounted on the church tower. The approach is without hazards, but a stern anchor should be ready before entering. Boats moor bow to pier, stern to anchor or sometimes alongside, but only in the outer basin (3.2m throughout), as the inner one is shoal. By late afternoon the harbour is often full, especially at weekends. Note that the S quay is reserved for the ferry. Water on the pier, and ancient but clean loos. There is a shop in the village close by. Beautiful bathing beach N of the harbour. Highly recommended out of season, but in July the hassle in the harbour rather spoils the pleasures of the beautiful surroundings.

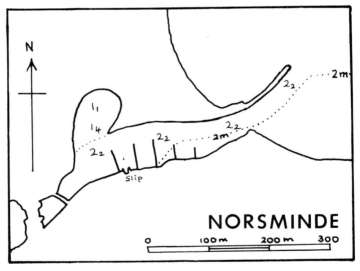

Norsminde   *see plan*

This small harbour S of Aarhus has 2.2m in the approach and along the S side of the harbour where the yacht jetties are; avoid the lagoon to the N, which is shoal. Look out for strong stream which can reach 3 knots running in or out. The entrance is liable to silting after E winds (in which some swell gets into the harbour); keep the outer pier just open on its S side on the approach. It is dangerous to attempt entry in strong onshore winds.

Water, diesel and simple stores available. Dues (1981) Kr30.

III · The Waters South of Fyn by the Store Baelt (Great Belt) to Sjaellands Odde

For cruise-planning chart and key to harbours covered, see combined chart at the beginning of Section II, on page 52.

Passage notes – Kieler Fjord to Aerø

This passage is quite straightforward, and I have only included this note in order to mention that it is unsafe to make for Marstal from the S in winds of over force 6 from S or SW. The sudden shoaling in the approach to the Klørdyb, the channel to Marstal, creates heavy seas under such conditions, and with the normal depth of only 2.4m I would avoid the attempt. Much better to round Skjoldnaes, the NW tip of Aerø, and fetch in perfect shelter down to Søby.

Dyreborg

A small square fishing harbour, clearly enough shown on chart 170. Keeping well over to the Bjørnø side, which is steep-to, the approach presents no problem and there is 2.5m everywhere within the harbour. There is mean tidal rise and fall of 0.9m, and NW winds can lower the level by up to a metre, so at LW with a strong NW wind there can be little more than 1 metre actual depth. The stern anchor should be made ready before entering as the harbour is often overcrowded, and it is wise to try to arrive early.

Dyreborg is worth visiting as it is a charming place set in wooded country. The loos are not bad, there is water on the quays, a kiosk in the harbour, and a shop in the village. Diesel is also available in the harbour. Dues (1981) Kr15.

Faaborg
see plan

This is a splendid place, and definitely not to be missed. There is a new yacht harbour to the NW of the old harbour, but the harbourmaster prefers visitors to try the old one first. There are guest pontoons in the N part of the basin; the S half is more fishing and commercial. Good showers (communal) and loos, and diesel is available alongside. There is a sailmaker, Sail Jack at Klostergade 13-15, and chandlers, the best being Bad og Motor beside the yacht harbour. This harbour has 206 berths and operates the green card system, so it is worth trying if the old harbour is very full (when I was there last they were suffering from a Naval visit!). Dues (1981) Kr40 for 8–12m, Kr50 12–16m.

The town is right next to the harbour and full of interesting things. Don't miss the bell tower in Taarngade, the remains of the town's first church: if you are feeling fit enough there is a wonderful view from the top. The church in Kirkestraede is also interesting, as are the old west gate and the old merchant's house preserved as a museum in Holkegade. There are beautiful old houses with courtyards, and do not miss my favourite – Kai Nielsen's sculpture Ymer's Well in Torvet, the main square, illustrating the Norse legend of the creation. With its convenience for shopping and interest as a town, Faaborg should if possible be dragged into any itinerary, and luckily it is well placed between the Little and Great Belts so most cruise tracks will pass somewhere nearby.

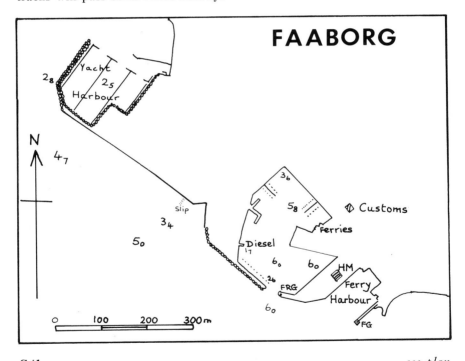

Søby
see plan

The least attractive of Aerø's three harbours, but usefully placed. The approach is easy except from the SE, when care must be taken to avoid the sands running $\frac{1}{2}$ mile offshore a mile SE of the entrance. Yachts lie either on the N wall of the N harbour (some swell in N winds), or (best berth but restricted room) on the wall E of the ferry berth in the S basin. Showers and loos just W of the ferry berth. Good Skibsproviant by S basin: food, charts and some chandlery. All stores in the village, 5 minutes away. No fuel. Dues

Faaborg from the clock tower

The museum courtyard in Faaborg

(1981) Kr40 for 8–10m, Kr48 10–15m. A noisy, restless place with heavy ferry traffic, but an invaluable refuge in heavy weather from S or W.

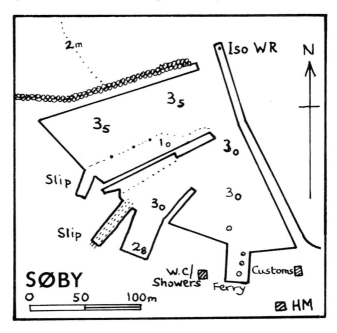

Fjaellebroen

see plan

This is a most alarming harbour to approach, as after the long (1 mile) buoyed approach the entrance is very narrow and invisible until you are almost in it: the entrance you *can* see is that to the dinghy harbour, which has only 1m depth inside. Steer for the starboard (SE) corner of the harbour

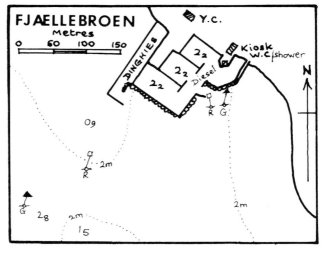

wall, and then to pass between the two channel buoys ENE of it before turning sharply to port to negotiate the entrance, which I estimate at just under 10m wide.

There is 2.2m depth in the approach and the same inside: moor as space allows. Water on the pontoons, fuel on the short pier projecting from the NE quay. There is a kiosk with a fair stock of food such as bread, milk and sausages, and primitive but clean loos and showers behind. Shop 100m away, which my notes record 'sells beer' – I think I had run out! There is a clubhouse, but when I was there it was shut except for the entrance hall where there is a telephone. W winds can lower the water level by up to 1m. Dues (1981) Kr25 for 8–10m, Kr30 over. A quiet little place, pleasant enough but of no great interest to the sightseer.

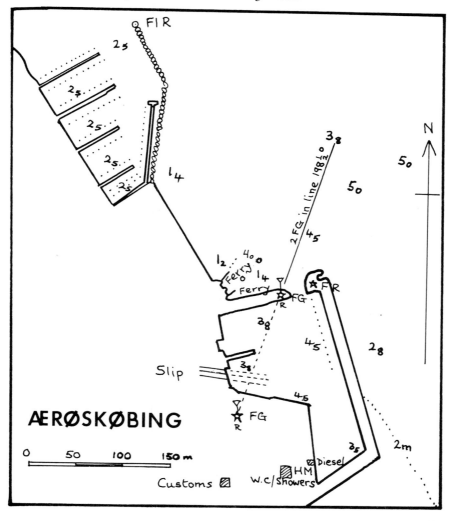

ÆRØSKØBING

Aerøskøbing

see plan

One of the most delightful towns in all Denmark, although the harbour tends to be crowded and it is always well to arrive early. Although the harbourmaster rather prefers visitors to use up the spare berths in the yacht harbour first, visiting yachts can also berth alongside in the old harbour, and as long as a decent position is available this is much more convenient than the grand new yacht harbour to the NW. If going into the latter note that the water is shoal from about 30m NW of the mole head. Dues (1981) Kr33 up to 10m, Kr45 10–15m.

The best showers are at the new harbour, loos at both. Diesel below the office in the old harbour: ask harbourmaster for service. All repairs except sails, excellent shopping within minutes of the harbour.

The town itself is the most important thing to see, but in particular one should visit the Peter Jacobsen Museum with its collection of ships in bottles, all made by him between 1887 and 1957 (he died in 1960 at 84, and liked to say that he had consumed the contents of all the bottles himself – except the milk ones!). The museum also has some lovely china dogs. And don't miss the eighteenth century church, which the brochures hardly mention. It has a very strange and powerful Crucifixion and a lovely carved pulpit, also several votive ship models including one of the famous English clipper *Thermopylae*.

A street in Aerøskøbing

Passage notes – The channels N and E of Aerø

This is a complex area, and navigation can be tricky in reduced visibility. Aerø and Fyn are separated by a line of islands and shoals, with a wide and easy channel W of Avernakø leading to Faaborg by a main channel W of Bjornø, or the more difficult Grydeløb, marked by four rather small buoys, E of Bjornø. Then there is a channel E of Avernakø, easily found as it is buoyed and the E point of the island has only a cable of shoal water extending from it. And finally, between Drejø and Hjortø is the well-buoyed Hojestene Løb, the main route from Aerøskøbing or Marstal to Svendborg. In poor visibility, a yacht of moderate draft can locate and steer for the ferry pier on Drejø, from where a course of 90° Mag. will bring the boat to the red can buoy which is the first marker of the channel.

Coming N from Marstal, few yachts need follow the main 3.8m channel as it bears E: a course of 33° Mag. from the N cardinal buoy at the N end of the Marstal approach channel, a mile N of the harbour entrance, cuts into the Mørkedyb with never less than 3m depth. The Kløbrdyb approach from the S has already been dealt with in Passage Notes for Kiel to Aerø earlier in this section: the SE coast of Aerø is fairly steep-to, so in poor visibility with smooth seas it is safe to steer E along the S Aerø coast about $\frac{1}{4}$ mile off, and then steer 50° Mag. from where it runs out, which leads into the closely buoyed Kløbrdyb in no less than 2m of water.

Sailing N via Rudkøbing, the special chart for the area of that town is not really needed. The red and white buoys at the ends of the channel leading through past Rudkøbing are shown on chart 170, and the channels are closely buoyed between those limits. The same applies to chart 171, covering the detail of the narrows of the channel past Svendborg and out into the open water between Fyn and Langeland.

Marstal   *see plan*

A remarkable harbour and a charming town, but unfortunately it seems to be on the way from everywhere to everywhere else so the harbour tends to be very overcrowded.

The approaches have been covered in the preceding Passage Notes. The main yacht berths are at the S end of the long harbour and there is also a small-boat harbour (2m) near the N end; otherwise it is a case of catch as catch can. There is a mean tidal range of 0.5m, and gales from the S quadrant can lower the mean level by up to 1.2m, which leaves very little water in the yacht basins, though still 2m or more along the main quays.

There are two lots of loos and showers at the S end, one just behind the yacht club, and loos by the boat harbour at the N end. Water on pontoons, diesel from Gulf station near the entrance at the N end of the harbour.

The town is beautiful and provides good shopping. The eighteenth century church is pretty, with an exceptional collection of votive ships and other treasures including a pair of candlesticks looted by a local sailor from a temple in Peking. The museum is also well worth a visit, with a fine

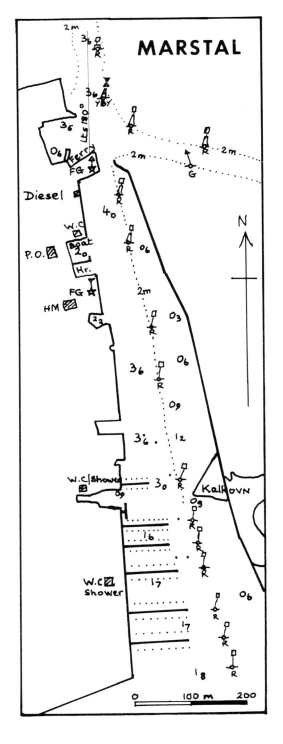

maritime collection.

The protective wall which forms the harbour was built by local sailors in the winters, using stones brought back by ships returning in ballast. The work started in the late eighteenth century and went on well into the nineteenth. Its survival is a tribute to the quality of the drystone techniques used, still clearly visible today.

Marstal

The tiny harbour on Hjortø

93

Hjortø

The harbour measures only 20m by 25m but is well worth visiting for a few hours to explore this pretty island. The channel is well marked and the harbour has mostly 1.8m. One must enter with caution as there is no room to manoeuvre. There is a small shop at the far end of the village, open 8–12 and 2–6, and a pretty basic loo by the harbour, otherwise no facilities. A daily ferry runs to Svendborg: its berth must be kept clear. Good bathing.

Svendborg   *see plan*

This fine town has surprisingly poor facilities for visiting yachts. Look out for swirls in the sound approaching the town: they can totally confuse an autopilot.

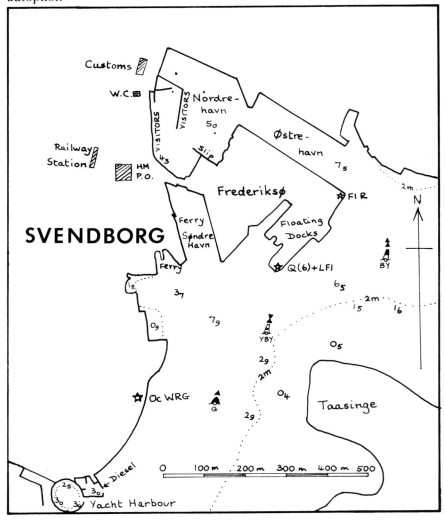

There is a large circular marina and fuel can be bought there at the entrance to the E basin, but there is seldom much room and visitors are advised to use the Nordrehavn. This is commercial and rather dirty, with dreadful loos and showers at its NW corner. The town lies just through the railway station, which is visible from the harbour, and much better loos can be found there. Excellent shopping and good rail connections. Repair facilities. The dues struck me as a bit steep: Kr30 up to 9m, Kr40 9–12m, Kr55 12–15m in 1981, for really very little. Our Lady's Church is worth seeing: originally Romanesque, it was partly rebuilt into cruciform Gothic and it has a carillon which plays four times a day. The town's oldest church, St Nikolaj (twelfth century Romanesque) is also not to be missed. But on the whole I would not go out of my way to visit Svendborg unless I wanted to put a crew-member on a train: I much prefer the E route via Rudkøbing.

Rudkøbing   *see plan*

This pleasant town on the W coast of Langeland lies on a well-buoyed channel and the approach is simple, although coming from the N care must be taken to round the S cardinal buoy off the Fiskerihavn before turning E for the Lystbaadehavn. Visitors berth in the yacht harbour if room,

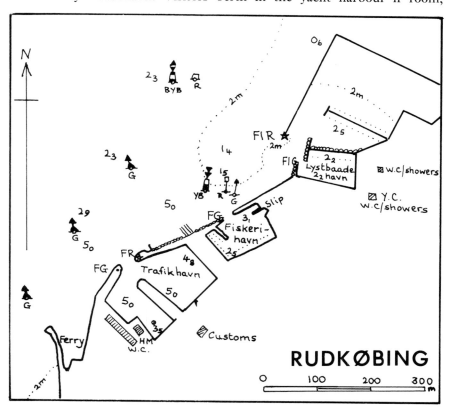

Rudkøbing is visible through the pillars of the Langeland bridge

Young people doing a little ship-repair job in Rudkøbing

otherwise overflow into first the Fiskerihavn and then the Trafikhavn, the latter being the more comfortable. There are good loos and showers in the clubhouse by the yacht harbour, and smaller ones in a nearby hut to the NW; truly awful public loos behind the harbour office on the SW wall of the SW Trafikhavn basin. Fibreglass repairs can be done by Bianca, near the yacht harbour. Dues (1981) Kr30 for 7–10m, Kr40 10–15m.

The old town is beautiful and unspoiled, like Aerøskøbing without the trippers. The Langeland Museum should be visited, and the early seventeenth century Late Romanesque church.

Bagenkop
see plan

Although on the W coast of Langeland, this harbour is the nearest Danish harbour to the Kieler Fjord and can be used as a passage port when going up the main Great Belt, E of Langeland, as well as by those bound for Rudkøbing, as it is only a couple of miles from the S point of Langeland. The approach can be rough in W winds.

Perhaps because the dues are relatively high, there always seems to be plenty of room here, and it is an excellent place for stocking up on supplies. Visitors berth in basin 3, and there are good loos at the S side of this basin behind the harbour office. There is a Marine Centre (repairs available) and a big Brugsen shop at the far corner of basin 1, and a baker and a butcher SE of the harbour near the church as well as a not very jolly looking *kro*. Diesel is available on the pier E of basin 1, and also that dividing basins 2 and 3.

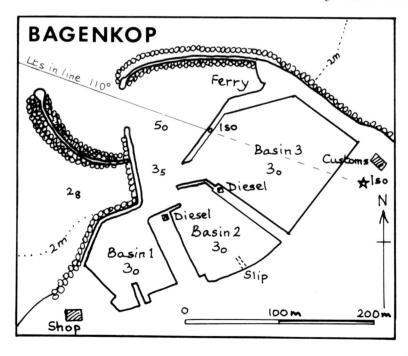

97

Dues in 1981 were among the highest in Denmark: Kr50 for 8–10m, Kr60 10–15m.

Nakskov Fjord

Here again the special chart (144) is not really needed: the entrance channel is marked on chart 142, and the rest of the way in is closely buoyed and can hardly be missed. With the plans provided here it is easy to reach any of the harbours of the fjord. It is an interesting area and worth a visit in spite of being rather out of the way, the numerous well-wooded islets giving it a character of its own.

Albuen   *see plan*

This is a very tricky place to enter, and should not be attempted if there is any swell running. I found a least depth of 5½ft (1.7m) in the approach round the point, but I understand that if the best line is found there is 2m. Once inside, keep a lookout from the bow as there are unmarked rocks, but the shelter is perfect and the water clear so these can be seen. Moor to the yacht jetty. No facilities. A wonderful place for a picnic and a swim (it is a recognised nudist beach).

Langø   *see plan*

This small harbour on the S side of the Nakskov Fjord makes a convenient overnight stopping place as it is fairly near the mouth of the fjord. The approach channel from the main channel is buoyed, and there are also good conspicuous N and S cone leading marks easily visible from the main channel. Berth as space allows. There is a shop whose owner speaks some English and provides diesel. For years a swallow has nested at head height in the porch of the shop, apparently quite unworried by customers. Reasonable loos, water from adjacent tap and long hose. Kiosk. A pleasant little working harbour, mostly fishing boats.

Hestehoved Yacht Harbour

The outline of this harbour is clearly marked on chart 142 on the N shore of the fjord in longitude 11° 05.7′E. There are two lateral buoys just outside the entrance. Engaged berths are marked red, free ones here have a white marker with the owner's date of return in red. This is the yacht harbour for Nakskov and the best place to stay a night, perhaps before sailing up to the town quay to explore and shop. Hot showers, kiosk, restaurant. No dues in 1981.

Nakskov

The town and harbour lie at the head of the fjord. Continue past the harbour office and do not berth until E of the small but pronounced elbow in the quay: yachts may lie anywhere E of this as space allows. Pretty awful showers and loos in a sort of seamen's home, part of the harbour offices

Bagenkop church

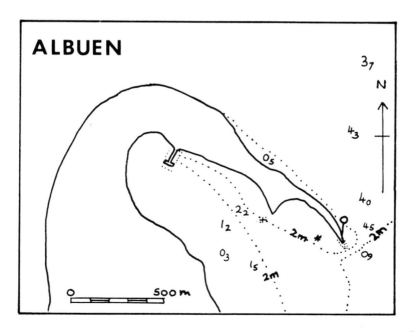

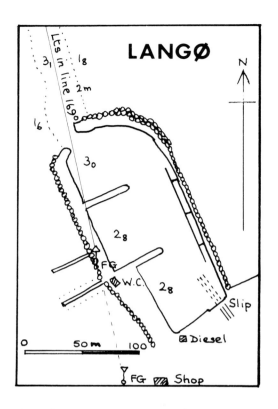

Town quay, Nakskov

building: unsuitable for lady crew members! The berth is very convenient to the excellent shops.

The town has some beautiful old streets, and do not miss St Nikolaj Church, a beautiful Late Gothic building with carved pulpit, 1657 altarpiece, lovely old family pictures, and where they still preserve the cannonballs that came in through the roof when the Swedes attacked in 1659. A thoroughly interesting and unusual town.

Taars

The small fishing harbour is ½ mile NW of the large ferry harbour. Enter by the buoyed ferry channel (keeping clear of ferries) and stay in the main channel until the leading marks for the fishing harbour come in line rather abaft the port beam, then turn onto that line. The harbour has 2m depth, reduced by up to 0.6m by SW gales. It is about 50m square, and there is often no room as there is an active fishing fleet. There are very communal loos and shower, small yacht club, tiny kiosk, otherwise stores from Sandby, 2½ miles: bicycles lent free of charge. Nasty swell in winds from S to W. A pretty area.

Taars: there is not much room for visitors

Onsevig

It can be impossible to find a berth in this small pier-end harbour, much of which is shoal. The 2m depth in most of the basin can fall to 1.3m in strong SW winds. Berth in any free slot. Loos and showers, water on quay in front of fish hall. The kiosk carries a few simple stores and there is a nice looking *kro* 300m up the road.

Spodsbjerg
see plan

This small E Langeland harbour is the only one on this side of the island and therefore tends to severe overcrowding. I have spent a perfectly comfortable night in a W wind force 4–5 anchored some 3 cables S of the entrance in 3m: if trying this, get well to the S to avoid being disturbed by wash from the heavy ferry traffic.

Best chance of a berth is on the S pier; diesel from tank near the head of the N mole. Fairly awful loos – chemical, I think. Kiosk over the road from the harbour, supermarket 500m away. Dues (1981) Kr30 over 8m.

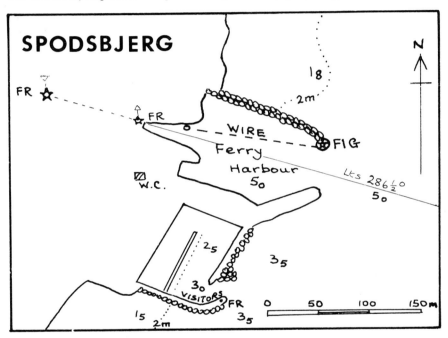

Dageløkke
This small marina on the W coast of Langeland is uncomfortable in W winds. Most of the basin has at least 2.5m and only the NW corner is shoal. The water level can fall by up to 0.9m in S to SE winds. Berths as space allows: best to arrive early in season to be sure of a berth. Good loos and showers, water on jetties, fuel, crane. Some simple stores available. Dues (1981) Kr35 for 7–9m, Kr40 9–12m. I would not recommend this port except on passage.

Lundeborg
A small harbour and suffers from severe overcrowding. The inner N basin is filled with fishing boats, leaving the S and outer basins for yachts: in season, arrive early to have a hope of a berth. Diesel on the central pier; its office is opposite the root of the pier. Water near diesel. Basic loos and showers,

kiosk, small shop 200m away. *Kro* near the harbour, fresh fish market in the harbour. Repairs to wooden hulls only from Baadbyggeri. Dues in 1981 were Kr30 for small boats, Kr45 for large: the harbourmaster decided which were which!

Lundeborg harbour. Do not rely on getting a berth.

Lohals
see plan

Approached by a buoyed channel through the offshore shoals: at night the white sector of the light leads in. It is also possible to approach from the N, perhaps from Omø or Skaelskør, keeping a mile off while rounding Hov and then closing to ½ mile offshore down the W coast of Langeland. Note Lohals Hage, the sandspit N of the harbour, marked by a red can buoy (Fl R 5s).

The large yacht harbour S of the commercial harbour is often full, in which case visitors must berth alongside in the old harbour as opportunity offers. Watch out for the ferry, which completely closes the entrance to the commercial harbour when berthed.

Dues (1981) Kr35 for 7–9m, Kr45 9–11m, Kr55 11–15m. Pretty basic showers and loos at both harbours. All provisions in Søndergade, and a good chandler in the village. Diesel in cans (and loan of wheelbarrow) from Gulf station in old harbour. Very pretty wooded surroundings and good bathing near the harbour.

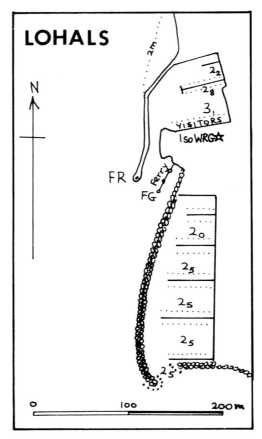

Omø *see plan*

A famous beauty-spot. The small size of the harbour ensures that it is overcrowded throughout the high season and at weekends during the rest of the summer. Indeed the harbourmaster actually tried to persuade me to omit his harbour from this book altogether! It would be a grave pity to do that, but what I will say is that of the 3000 arrivals every season, 500 have to be turned away because the harbour can take a maximum of only 90 boats, so visitors should aim to arrive before 1600 to have a reasonable certainty of a berth.

Diesel is available alongside on the W quay, water tap by the slip. Small but clean loos at the end of the E pier, also phone box. Fresh fish can be bought in the harbour. The village is a nice walk of about $\frac{3}{4}$ mile and simple stores are available there, also a bank. The island has charming walks and good bathing. Dues (1981) Kr30 for 8–10m, Kr40 10–15. If the harbour is full, sheltered anchorage in winds between SW and N can be found on the E side of the island (after rounding Omø Rev) S of the 24m peak of Skovbanke in 5–6m.

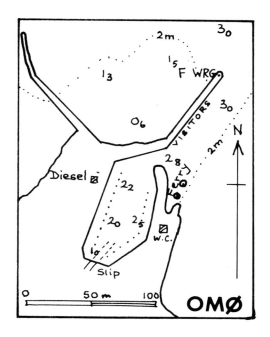

Skaelskør from the bridge. Note the vicious stream in the inner harbour (foreground).

Agersø

This has always seemed to me an excellent alternative to Omø. The area is very pretty but the island is less praised in the literature, with the result that the harbour does not fill up nearly so early and there is generally room at any hour.

The approach from Agersø Sund is straightforward and visitors berth as space permits. Diesel is available, and there is a water hose. The nice sprawly town has the biggest duckpond I have ever seen. There is a baker near the harbour, other shops and bank ten minute's walk. Lovely walks along the coast N and S of the harbour. Dues (1981) Kr30 for 8–12m, Kr40 12–15m.

Skaelskør
see inset on chart 160

As clearly shown on the chart 160 inset, the approaches to this harbour are well marked, but it must never be forgotten that the stream into and out of the fjord can reach 5 knots. This is mainly tidal, although the rise and fall

Nyborg is well equipped for all repairs. This machine enabled a quick repair to be made to a broken spreader.

View from Nyborg Castle

averages only 0.5m, and therefore it may be expected to be at its worst near springs. Yachts berth in the Lystbaadehavn on the N bank near the W end of the town. No dues in 1981.

Diesel beside slip, tiny but nice loo in yacht club. Torbensbaadeservice can do engine and fibreglass or wooden hull repairs, and the owner speaks good English. Sailmaker in Maglebyvej. There are shops near the yacht harbour, though the main town is over the bridge on the south bank. The church is on the N side near the yacht harbour and dates from the thirteenth century. It has a nice carved pulpit and a fifteenth century painted relief altarpiece, also a good votive ship. A pleasant place for those prepared to go off the beaten track.

Warning: It is dangerous to enter the Inderhavn on an ingoing stream, as the average yacht will risk being swept onto the bridge before she can manoeuvre.

Nyborg
see inset on chart 142

A major ferry, commercial and yacht port on the main Esbjerg–Copenhagen line, and convenient for changing crews.

The approach is to the W of a new breakwater, which protects small boats from the wash from heavy ferry traffic (and the ferries from idiots getting under their bows!). The channel is well marked by day or night. Visitors should berth in the new yacht harbour, the first basin on the port hand. The green/red cards revolve, with free berths showing green uppermost. Water and electricity on the jetties, diesel in the NW corner of the Østerhavn. Small shop and baker near harbour, nearest supermarket 10 minutes away, better shops a little farther. Sailmaker in Søndergade. Alubaat have excellent and relatively cheap repair capabilities: they have a sort of pulpit on a hydraulic arm fitted to a tractor that enables them to make mast repairs without lowering the spar.

The thirteenth century castle is surrounded by beautiful buildings and is well worth a visit; it has a very early painted wall decoration and interesting collections of arms, armour, furniture and pictures. There is also a nice church with fine early paintings on family memorials, and a fascinating three-masted votive ship with funnel and propeller. Dues (1981) Kr35 for 8–12m, Kr50 over.

Korsør

This busy ferry port has a splendid modern marina with its own entrance S of the commercial harbour: the old yacht basin in the main harbour is now closed. The approach to the marina runs NE from the W cardinal buoy marking the Badstue Rev, leaving two green conical buoys to starboard. There is a minimum of 2.4m on the jetties, but do not go up into the NE part of the harbour which is shoal. Water and electricity on the jetties, diesel pump (closed 12–2). The harbourmaster speaks good English and will advise. His office near the root of the S breakwater has good showers and loos, and also a restaurant which is rather expensive but good. There is a chandler nearby, open weekends too; shops are 5 minutes from the yacht harbour. Some repairs available in the Fiskerihavn (main harbour).

Korsør is an ancient ferry town, having depended on ferry traffic since the eleventh century, and it has some beautiful old streets (look for Rosenstraede) and buildings, notably Kongegaarden in Algade where the Danish kings used to stay if the Great Belt was too rough to cross when they arrived. Tourists tend to pass through without stopping, but I have always thought it a pleasant place, well worth a visit in its own right.

Kerteminde   *see plan*

Lying at the head of a deep bay, Kerteminde has a commercial harbour and a new marina to its N. The most convenient berths, and in more interesting surroundings, are to be found alongside in the old harbour, but beware of the stream. NW to NE winds produce a strong ingoing stream, and it is vital for yachts to turn head-to-stream in good time before the narrows at the W end of the basin or they risk being swept up into the bridge: in a light northerly I measured $1\frac{1}{2}$ knots of ingoing stream here. There is 0.5m rise

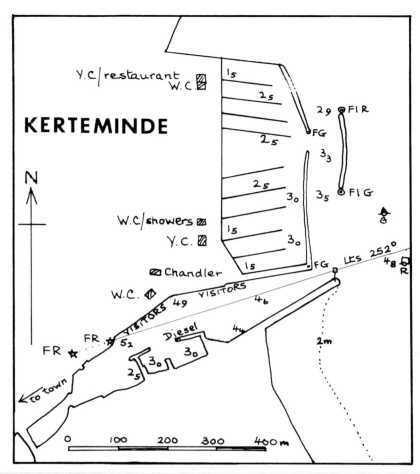

The anchorage at Musholm

and fall at mean tides, and S winds can lower the water level by up to 0.8m, which leaves only 1.5m depth at LW at the jetty ends in the yacht harbour, and less near the roots. There is always plenty of depth for yachts in the old harbour.

Baadkommissaeren, between the two harbours, has excellent chandlery and can do all repairs: a sailmaker collects every evening and returns next day. There are rather poor loos at the old harbour, much better ones at the two yacht clubs at the S and N ends of the yacht harbour; both have restaurant facilities. The old harbour suffers from swell in E winds.

A diesel tanker lorry supplies the marina every day 0800–1000; there is also a diesel pump on the E pierhead of the Fiskerihavn on the S bank of the old harbour. Look out for swirls near the entrance due to stream.

Kerteminde is a lovely old town with many old buildings, often in commercial use, and one of the banks occupies a particularly pretty one. The church dates from 1200 and is worth a visit, as is the museum (closed Mondays). Dues (1981) Kr35 for any size.

Musholm Havn
An idyllic little natural harbour formed by a tiny island lying 2 miles off the Sjaelland shore. The whole E side of the island forms a bay, with an inlet at its S end where a small jetty will be found. Moor bow to jetty stern to post, or lie to mooring buoy or anchor in the bay beyond, 2m depth. Some swell gets in in strong NE winds. No facilities, but super bathing and very pretty.

Mullerup   *see plan*
This small marina is owned by BP, whose station is open 0800–1700 every day. It has water on all jetties and a 25 ton Travellift, the use of which costs Kr300. Dues (1981) Kr25 for 7–10m, Kr35 over. A small boat builder, Coronet, can do minor repairs. Small nasty loos and showers. A small shop was expected to open during 1982, otherwise stores from the village, over a mile. A dull but useful passage port, space usually available.

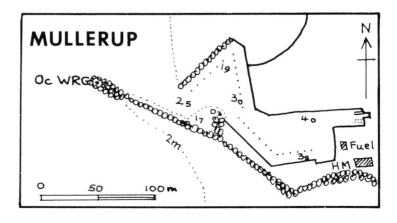

Reersø is charming even in the rain!

Reersø

A small fishing port on a peninsula on Sjaelland and not well known, but it is a favourite of mine and well worth a visit. The approach is simple and berthing is alongside as space allows. The tiny harbour loo is OK, and there is a fish market nearby. The harbour and its area is rather dull but the village (800m away though there is a self-service store about 500m from the harbour) is charming and well worth exploring. It has a good baker, general store and *kro*, which is in one of the many delightful old buildings. There is a fish smokery, and an ancient race of tailless cats. Dues (1981) Kr25 up to 8m, Kr30 over.

Korshavn   *see plan*

A beautiful natural harbour on the NE tip of Fyn. Note that, as the plan shows, it is not safe to round Fyns Hoved and then steer straight for the entrance buoys: one must get a good $\frac{1}{2}$ mile W of Fyns Hoved and then steer no less than 185° Mag. until the buoys are abeam before turning into the entrance channel. Approach then on the line of the leading beacons until 200m offshore, after which the point can be rounded into the harbour. There is 2.6m at the jetty end, less inshore. There are stern buoys for the outer jetty, posts for the inner berths. Dues (1981) Kr30 up to 9m, Kr40

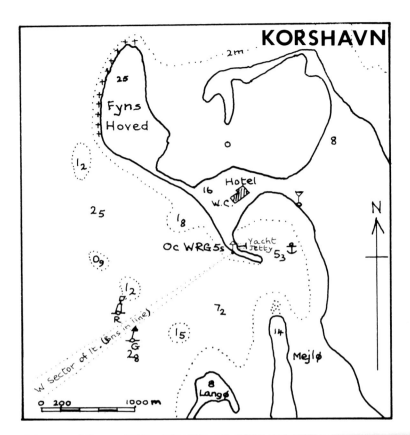

Rounding the sand-spit to enter Korshavn

Egensedybet yacht harbour in Odense Fjord

over. Water on jetty. There is a hotel and restaurant (visitors may use its jetty) and public loos. Showers and shops at camping site 800m away.

The buoys in the bight are private, but one may anchor: however, the holding is soft mud, and I dragged a 25lb CQR in a wind of only force 4–5, and had to get out my 35lb bower, so be sure to use adequate ground tackle. An excellent passage port and a charming place with good swimming.

Otterup (Egensedybet Lystbaadehavn)
This small marina up a side branch of the Odense fjord is a nice little place, and the approaches are easy as long as chart 115 is carried, which is needed for any visit to the Odense Fjord. The harbour has 2.5m. There is water on the jetties, a sailmaker in the village (7km), and the harbour has very good showers and loos and a beautiful clubhouse. Nearest shop 3km.

Odense
see inset on chart 115

An ancient and beautiful town, the birthplace of Hans Christian Andersen. Odense is well worth a visit for the touristically inclined, in spite of the fact that it lies some 12 miles up the fjord from its entrance and even further from the ordinary cruising routes. Chart 115 must be carried.

There is a yacht harbour for the locals at Stige, but as this is 2 miles N of Odense it is not much use to visitors, who mostly berth at the S end of basin 3, unless there is room on the yacht jetty NW of there. The approach through the fjord is heavily buoyed and quite simple: the scenery is unfortunately spoiled by the huge commercial port of Lindøvaerftet in the middle. Among the many sights worth seeing are St Knud's Cathedral (thirteenth century with perhaps the most beautiful altarpiece in Scandinavia, by Claus Berg), St Hans Church because of its extraordinary exterior pulpit, Hans Anderson's house in Hans Jensensstraede and his childhood home in Munkmøllestraede, the DSB railway museum near the harbour with a large working model railway, and many beautiful old buildings especially in Jernbanegade (in spite of its modern name) and Albani Torvet where the splendidly named Home for Unmarried Gentlewomen is to be found. All supplies, though the town centre is $\frac{3}{4}$ mile from the recommended berths.

Kalundborg *see plan*

Entering the fjord in strong W winds, be sure to keep well N of Asnaes as the seas break heavily over Asnaes NW Flak. Otherwise the approach is straightforward and the entrance is well marked. Yachts berth in the

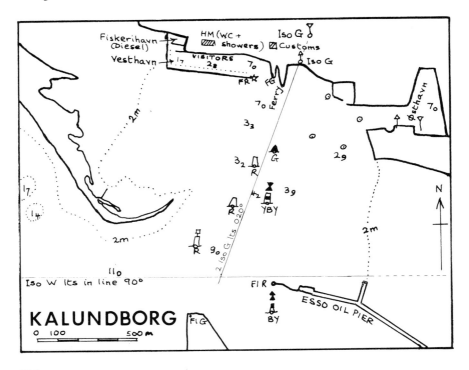

Kalundborg. The beautiful five-spired church dominates the Vesthavn.

Vesthavn, green cards for free berths, or there is usually plenty of room to lie alongside the N wall. Dues (1981) Kr25 up to 12m, Kr35 over. Loos and old but spacious showers under harbour office, also phone. Diesel in Fiskerihavn: apply to harbourmaster for service. He is friendly and speaks good English. Small repair shop and chandler, no sailmaker.

Excellent shopping close to the harbour. I enjoyed the museum in Lindegaarden with period interiors, and the church with its five spires is extraordinary – though not unique: there is another in Doornik in Belgium built at almost the same date. It seems to have a very small interior for such a massive building, but it contains a marvellous naive, brightly painted altarpiece (1650) which includes Adam with a goatee beard, Moses carrying a set of ready-numbered Commandments, and splendidly scarlet-cheeked angels and cherubim. Well worth the detour.

Ballen   *see plan*

This useful harbour on the E coast of Samsø is often overcrowded, but in that case good anchorage can be found in the area N of the outer half of the N breakwater in 3–4m, good holding in sand and mud. Berth as space permits (if it does!): an area of the S wall is reserved for fishing boats, while the Fiskerihavn although still so called is now for yachts only. Diesel from pump on N side of Fiskerihavn entrance, water and electricity. Shops very close to harbour. Good though rather dear restaurant N of central Fiskerihavn, good loos and shower N of its W tip. There is also a dreadful loo in the side of the harbour office, at the S side of the Fiskerihavn, which is open 24 hours a day: the others close at night. The shop up the road from the Fiskerihavn serves the diesel pump.

A good place to arrive late, anchor overnight outside (except of course in winds with an easterly component) and then come in, berth and shop next day.

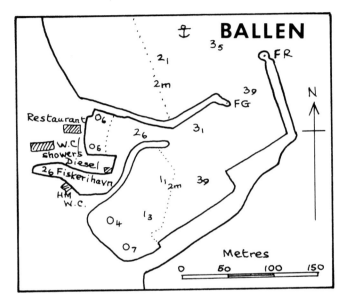

Langør
see plan

A small landlocked harbour in Stavns Fjord on the E side of Samsø. The approach from the E via Lindhom Løb is tricky: experienced mud-hoppers can cut across from the red buoy off Kyholm, making good 260° Mag. until the green buoy off Armhoved bears S, and then turning onto a course to leave it close to starboard. I found no less than 2.5m depth on this track, but it is safer to go out by Kyholm Løb, leaving the E cardinal buoy close to port, and then return round the N side of the Kyholm Bo N cardinal buoy, S between the two lateral buoys, and then on S to the green buoy off Armhoved mentioned above. In either case steer from this buoy until the second (SW) point of Armhoved is open of the first, when it is safe to steer direct for the harbour.

Visitors lie mostly on the outside of the two breakwaters that form the harbour; there is room to lie outside the W wall but inside the outer mole of boulders. There is also good anchorage in the bay NE of the harbour, between the two points of Armhoved. Good showers and loos, shop 100m up the road which can also supply diesel in cans. Kiosk in the harbour. A

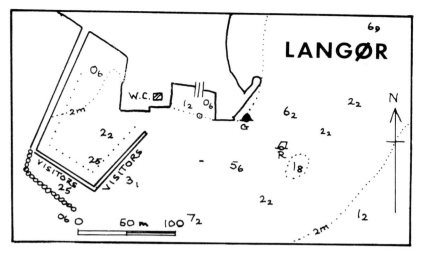

wild and beautiful area, well worth visiting.

Røsnaes

This small fishing harbour lies at the end of a long pier about 3 miles E of Røsnaes Point. Approach to the E of the pierhead, as the entrance faces E. There is 2.8m everywhere in the little basin. Diesel available, water and primitive loos. Considerable swell in E winds, and the harbour can be crowded with fishing boats: only use if unavoidable.

Sejerø

The harbour lies at about the centre of the SW coast of this pretty island and gets some swell in strong S winds. The approach is straightforward. Berth as space allows or as instructed: the harbourmaster is energetic and directs by vigorous gestures (no English). Do not attempt to enter the tiny boat harbour E of the main entrance without local advice.

Diesel from N side of entrance: the harbourmaster will arrange service, or failing him enquire at the shop. A baker's van arrives at the harbour 0845. First-class loos and showers. There are bus tours round the island starting from the ferry station, and visiting the barrow at its E end, which I hear are well worth taking though alas I have never had time. A thoroughly nice friendly place with good bathing beaches and a pretty church in the town. Dues (1981) Kr35 up to 10m, then Kr5 for each extra metre.

Nekselø

A jetty on the E side of the island, clearly marked on chart 103. It has 2m near the end and is in a perfectly idyllic setting. There is room for only about three boats, and it is open to winds between NE and E, but in suitable weather it is a most beautiful place for a picnic, or even to stay a night in really settled weather. No facilities, no dues.

The idyllic jetty mooring at Nekselø

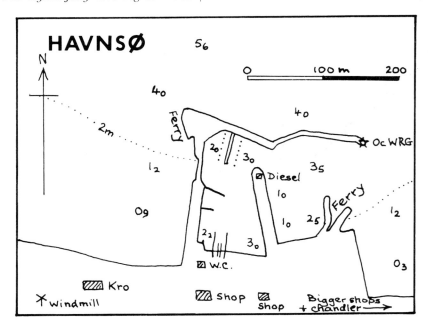

Havnsø   *see plan*

A little harbour rather off the beaten track, but it is a genuine and unusual place and I enjoyed my visit. Visitors berth in the W basin as space permits. Fuel pumps on centre mole, and there is a chandler close to the harbour up the road to the E, with reasonable stocks of charts. There are small but adequate loos and two shops near the harbour, supermarket beyond the chandler and *kro* by the windmill just W of the harbour. Dues (1981) Kr35 up to 10m, plus Kr5 for each additional metre.

Passage notes – Sjaellands Odde

Sailing between the Samsø Belt and Hesselø Bugt involves rounding the dramatic peninsula of Sjaellands Odde. This consists of a narrow spit of land some 10 miles long, extended by a shoal that continues in roughly the same direction for another 5 miles. However, about $1\frac{1}{2}$ miles NNW from the end of the land there is a gap in the shoal, the Snekkeløb, marked by a green and a red buoy, the green one to be left to port and the red to starboard when going E, and vice versa. This passage is safe in any normal conditions as long as the buoys have been identified, but they are rather small and can be difficult to find in heavy seas. There is an even narrower gap in the shoal halfway between the end of the land and the Snekkeløb, marked according to the chart by a red buoy: this is called Baadeløbet (the boat passage) and I must confess I have never seen this buoy, which is probably very small. I would not recommend anyone to try this latter passage, but if any reader does (only under ideal conditions, I would suggest!) I would be glad to hear all about it.

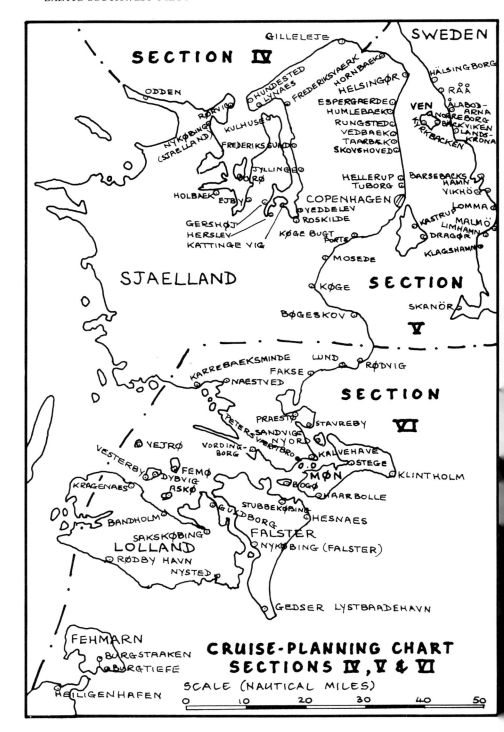

CRUISE-PLANNING CHART
SECTIONS IV, V & VI
SCALE (NAUTICAL MILES)

IV · Sjaellands Odde to Gilleleje

Passage notes – North Sjaelland
There is very little to say about this passage as almost all of it is straightforward for yachts of normal draft. There is a shoal with less than 3m depth extending over a mile N from the W side of the entrance to the Isefjord. For boats entering the Isefjord there is an inshore passage marked by a S cardinal buoy about 4 cables N of Korshage: if a yacht passes close S of this buoy and thereafter keeps parallel to the shore as it curls round to the S, this leads safely down into the Vesterløb and so into the fjord without the need to round the shoal to the N.

Odden *see plan*
This port is of little intrinsic interest, but it has vital strategic importance as the only port between Sjaellands Odde and the Isefjord. Visitors mostly berth on the S side of the outer breakwater, as far W as space permits: always plenty of room. There are nice small loos and (communal) showers. Diesel is available at the fish auction hall, 1000–1100 only and not Sundays. Odden Baadevaerft do motor and fibreglass or wooden hull repairs, and have good stocks of charts. They are also scuba equipment and repair specialists. Fresh and smoked fish on sale in the harbour, which is a major fishing port. Water only in the NW corner of the W basin and near the fish hall. Small shop near the harbour; the main town is about 15 minutes for a fit person, straight up the steep hill, and has a baker, banks and several shops.

I have to admit that my most lasting memory of this useful harbour is of the all-pervading smell of drains.

The Isefjord and Roskildefjord
This great body of water running S deep into the centre of Sjaelland is little visited by foreign yachtsmen, which is a great pity as they miss some of the most beautiful scenery in Denmark. The Isefjord is wide, pastoral and pretty, the Roskildefjord narrower and in places breathtakingly beautiful. It would be easy to spend a fortnight or more cruising these waters without ever going out to sea, sleeping in a different port every night.

In contrast to many Danish fjords, the large-scale charts really are needed

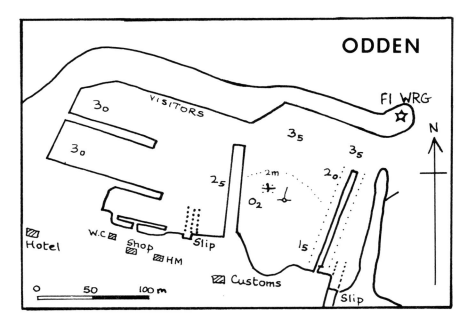

here: No.116 for the Isefjord and Nos.117 (N) and 118 (S) for the Roskildefjord. Navigation of the Isefjord is straightforward except for the channel E of Orø, which is unmarked and should only be attempted by experienced skippers, though it is prettier than the well-buoyed W route. Careful pilotage is needed in the Roskildefjord, particularly in its S reaches, but the channels though narrow are well marked and as long as concentration is kept at a high level there should really be no problems. Do try to visit both: but if a choice had to be made I would have to take the Roskildefjord, whose S reaches especially are among my favourite waters anywhere in Europe.

Rørvig *see inset on chart 116*

A very small and rather shallow harbour near the mouth of the Isefjord that can be useful for late arrivals. The stern anchor should be made ready before entering: boats lie bow to jetty and stern to anchor. Gales from between S and SE can lower the water level by over a metre, which would leave most yachts waiting for a change in the weather. Dues (1981) Kr25 up to 15m, Kr 50 over. Do not attempt the SW basin, which has a very narrow entrance and only 1.2m at ML.

There is a small yacht club and a kiosk, with the unusual combination of good showers and nasty loos beyond. A very good smoked and fresh fish shop also sells a little meat – try their delicious *fiskefrikadeller*. General shop 200m up the road. Water hose in SW corner of the harbour. The church, 2km to the W, originally belonged to the village of Isøre which was buried by the sand in 1527.

Nykøbing, Sjaelland   *see inset on chart 116*

The vast new yacht harbour is only partly shown on the inset: it lies W of the old harbour and extends W some 300m. Always plenty of room: dues (1981) Kr25 per boat. Fuel pumps at the W side of the entrance to the old harbour, closed 1100–1330. Yacht club, with cafeteria open 1000–2200. The town is about 500m away and has all stores including a bookshop with very good stocks of charts. The Odsherred Folk Museum with its interiors of workshops, bakery etc is worth visiting.

Orø

This small harbour on an idyllic island should be approached on a course between 90° and 100° Mag. There is 2.5m. depth except alongside the inner jetty, which has 2m. There is 0.5m rise and fall at mean tides, and SE winds can lower the mean level by up to 1m. Tiny but good loos, water, no fuel or repairs. When I was there in 1981 the harbourmaster spoke no English or German. The village $\frac{3}{4}$ mile away has two general stores and a very nice church with an outbuilding with a curious sculptured thatch roof. Many of the houses have red tile roofs with thatch overlaid. The island is pretty with maize fields and pine and beech woods: I would visit by day and spend the night at Holbaek. Dues (1981) Kr37 for 8–12m, Kr 55 12–14m. This covered three days, though few people could afford the time to stay that long and it seemed a bit steep for one night.

Rørvig: the departing ferry almost brushed past Kuri Moana

There is a pretty little yacht jetty on the mainland a mile WSW from Orø harbour, with 1.8m depth at its end. It is owned by Holbaek yacht club but guests are welcome as long as there is room, and it would be a charming place to spend a night in settled weather.

Holbaek
see inset on chart 116

Visitors are best advised to spend the night in the large marina 1½ miles E of the main harbour (and not included on the inset, but well shown on the main chart), but to explore the town one may berth in the Skibshavn. There are pile moorings on the NE wall, owned by Holbaek Baatcharter, who charge Kr25 per day (1981) if a space is free; plenty of room alongside elsewhere, but high dues as for Orø. There are loos W of the entrance, and a shower (key from Baatcharter). Nice old town, shops 200m away.

The yacht harbour is large, modern, shiny and (for the first week's stay, at least) free! Guest berths are on the S jetty. Huge grand clubhouse with bar, kiosk and restaurant, and luxurious loos and (highly communal) showers. The fuel berth is at the E end of the S wall, open only 1600–1900 Friday evenings and 1000–1300 Saturdays, Sundays and holidays. The club will advise on repairs or any other problems, and are extremely hospitable and helpful.

Ejby

This small harbour is privately owned and may therefore refuse admission if it is overcrowded, which it often is. There is only 1.5m in the entrance, and with a rise and fall of 0.5m and SE winds lowering the mean by up to 0.6m it is not for every boat, but there is always good anchorage in Bramsnaes Vig to the S, except in N winds. When I visited the harbour it was being used as a bathing pool by a group of rather yobbish young, and the basin is only big enough for three or four yachts, so on the whole I cannot really recommend a visit.

Kyndbyvaerket

A usefully placed harbour but unfortunately exclusively for vessels concerned with the electrical power station there, and yachts are not allowed to enter.

Lynaes

The harbour is clearly shown on chart 116, the W basin being the old harbour with the large yacht harbour to the E and N. Best to try the yacht harbour first, but if it's full one can always cram into the old harbour somewhere, though it gets very full at weekends. Toilets and showers at the top of the yacht harbour, also restaurant. Diesel at the NE entrance of the yacht harbour and also at the head of the old harbour, both open 9–11 and 2–4. All repairs including sailmaker, excellent food and chandlery in the harbour area. This is really the yacht port for Hundested and there is

Lynaes is the best harbour near the mouth of the Ise and Roskildefjords

relatively little commercial traffic. It is a happy, friendly place, although there is nothing of great interest beyond the harbour, and ideally placed as a passage port for coasting along N Sjaelland, or as a base from which to explore the Isefjord and Roskildefjord.

Hundested   *see inset on chart 116*

The main value of this harbour to the yachtsman is its ease of entry from seaward in the dark, and any stranger arriving at the Isefjord entrance in falling dark or later is well advised to enter here and wait for daylight before carrying on. The buoys are unlit but a yacht can safely keep 2 cables offshore, using the traffic in the buoyed channel as a guide. Yachts lie in the Sydhavnen as space allows. Swell in W winds.

Diesel from pump at the root of the S breakwater: arrange service at the office N of the E end of the S basin. Good loos and showers near the SE corner of the S basin. Fish shops in harbour, others 250m away. Motor repairs. Dues (1981) Kr25. Bathing beach N of harbour entrance. Lynaes is far preferable under ordinary circumstances. The famous Mølich yard will do all yacht repairs.

The museum of the Greenland explorer Knud Rasmussen in his old house beside the Spodsbjerg light is worth visiting.

Kulhuse

This small crowded harbour on the S side of the Roskildefjord entrance is constantly disturbed by ferry traffic. There is a yacht club and a *kro*, but there seems little point in using this particular harbour with Lynaes offering far more comfort nearby.

Frederiksvaerk   *see inset on chart 117*

A dirty, noisy industrial harbour where the locals tell me they have to wash their boats down with 10 per cent hydrochloric acid to remove the deposits from the steelworks! Visitors berth in the N harbour as space permits. Tap and hose, nice small loos in blue hut at end of harbour. There is a small engineer who is highly thought of; he also keeps charts.

Frederikssund Bridge

The bridge opens if needed every full and half hour between sunrise and sunset, usual signals. Passing through the old bridge further S, south-going boats pass between piles 4 and 5, north-going between piles 3 and 4, numbered from the W end of the bridge.

Frederikssund and Marbaek

There are two yacht harbours within the same basin S of the town, Frederikssund Lystbaadehavn being the larger one of the W side, with its jetties projecting E from the main breakwater, and Marbaek Lystbaadehavn on the E side, with jetties running out from the mainland. The joint entrance lies about ½ mile S of the old bridge. Coming from the N, most yachts can safely cut across the Kalvø Rev shoal that runs S from the breakwater just S of the first red buoy.

Frederikssund yacht harbour is rather bare and bleak but has plenty of room. Fuel on the northernmost jetty, service from the harbourmaster who closes down on Mondays and Tuesdays. There is a chandler and a clubhouse with loos and showers, cafeteria in the Hallen building, shops ¾ mile. Dues (1981) Kr20.

Marbaek has a fuel pump at the root of its central jetty, and a 20 ton Travellift. Fuel service from Marine Smeden, who also do motor and minor rigging repairs and have a sailmaker. They open 0900–2000 every day April–October, so fuel is always available this side, but note that the depth at the fuel jetty is only about 1.7m, with a 0.5m rise and fall, and ESE winds can lower the mean level by up to a metre. The harbour office with loos and showers and a chandlery lies just E of Marine Smeden's building. There is a wooden shipbuilder, who can repair wooden hulls. No dues for the first two days (1981), thereafter Kr50 per day.

Jyllinge Lystbaadehavn

A useful large yacht harbour about 5 miles S of Frederikssund and up a blind channel on the E side of the fjord, the main through route being down the W shore. There is water on all the jetties, and diesel is available 9–12 and 2–6, except Mondays. The harbour has 2m depth but SE winds can lower this by up to a metre. There is a 10 ton lift, chandlery, kiosk and cafeteria; the harbour loos are in the entrance of the latter. Small yacht club. Shops 800m away.

Østby
A private commercial harbour and should not be entered by yachts.

Veddelev
Located $1\frac{1}{2}$ miles N of Roskilde, this harbour contains many of the boats owned by inhabitants of the larger town, but visitors will usually prefer to berth nearer the attractions of Roskilde itself. Water, loos and clubhouse, no other facilities.

Roskilde   *see inset on chart 118*
This beautiful and ancient town has been the burial place of the Danish royal family since the middle ages, but there are more cheerful reasons for visiting it, too. Visitors berth in free berths (green card system) in the W basin, or alongside as space permits in the E one. Water on jetties, diesel and petrol at SE corner of E basin. Friendly yacht club with bar/restaurant: it has loos and there are others near the W basin. Shops are $\frac{1}{2}$ mile away just S

Roskilde. The longships museum is a model of its kind.

of the cathedral, but there is a *skibsproviant* with most stores beside the yacht club, just S of the E basin.

Sightseers must not miss the twelfth century cathedral with its rich treasures and royal tombs, and the palace close by built in 1733 for the Danish kings but now the Bishop's residence (open every day 1–4). Another must is the Viking Ship Museum near the harbour, beautifully laid out and a model of its kind. The old church of St Jørgensbjerg just above the harbour is also worth seeing, and there are wonderful views over the fjord from the park just N of this church.

Kattinge Vig
A beautiful natural harbour just NW of Roskilde which offers secure anchorage in any weather. The NW corner in about 3m, mud, is the best place except in SE winds when the bay to the S just after entering is more comfortable. Surrounded by wooded hills, this is a beautiful place to spend a night, perhaps after a day exploring Roskilde, and it contains Denmark's only 'atoll', a strange ring-shaped island probably formed as a result of mining some stone or mineral from its middle.

A fascinating old clock high up in Roskilde Cathedral

Gershøj

The approach to this part of the fjord is through a long reef: the best gap to use is the S one of the two buoyed passages. But navigate with care as the buoys are difficult to see among the fish stakes that clutter the area, and Nørrerev, although marked as an island on the chart, is so low that it can only be seen from very close.

The harbour itself is tiny, but there is room to lie on the wall outside, safe in all but strong easterlies as the water ½ mile offshore is shoal. A most pretty little village, with a little plum-coloured church that looks like a sugar-candy toy and contains a 1625 carved pulpit. This and the village shop are 100m from the quay. Do not miss this delightful place if you can help it, but readers who appreciate peace should avoid Friday, Saturday and Sunday nights when the local *kro* makes the air hideous with its disco.

Gershøj, a little-known and delightful spot near the head of the Roskildefjord

Herslev Lystbaadehavn

Clearly marked on chart 118, this small yacht harbour was recently built in one of the most beautiful situations you could ever wish to find. It has 1.8m depth and there is not a lot of room; green card system. No facilities except a water tap, and nice loos below the clubhouse which, if it is open, provides a splendid view of the fjord.

Passage note – Isefjord to Gilleleje

This 18 mile passage is covered only by the small-scale chart 102 until the approaches to Gilleleje are reached, when it is important to change to chart 131 which shows the shoals off Gilleleje more clearly. Fortunately the earlier part of the passage is quite without hazards, and it is safe to keep $\frac{1}{2}$ mile offshore all the way.

Gilleleje
see inset on chart 131

The offshore shoals are clearly marked on chart 131: coming from the W it is best to pass close S of the Vesterlands Grunde S cardinal buoy, then turn SE between the entrance buoys and so to the entrance. From the E, avoid passing over the Søborghoved Grund in heavy weather, as the sea can break badly over it. There are sometimes strong cross-seas in the entrance.

This is a popular fishing and yacht harbour, always rather crowded but another one can always cram in somewhere. Yachts berth as space allows in any of the basins except the Yderhavn. There are stern posts in the E basin (a long walk from town); in the two W basins boats lie to stern anchors or alongside according to position and the harbourmaster's instructions. Dues Kr25 up to 2m beam, plus Kr5 for each additional $\frac{1}{2}$m (1981); the harbour office opens 0700–0800, 1730–1830 and 1900–2100, and the rule is that anyone failing to come in and pay during the first available opening period after his arrival has to pay double. Water on all jetties, diesel in the NW corner of the S basin, office at the root of the short pier halfway down the W quay of that basin. Several loos, shower.

All repairs, two boatbuilders, engineer, sailmaker. Nice bustling little town, shops close to the harbour, and several (rather pricey) restaurants, many overlooking the harbour. Good bathing beaches all round. Veteran railway to Helsingør.

V · The Sound (Øresund), Gilleleje to Stevns Klint

For cruise-planning chart and key to harbours covered, see combined chart at beginning of Section IV, on page 120.

Hornbaek
see inset on chart 131

A pretty little town but the harbour tends to be severely overcrowded at weekends or in the holiday season. Approach by the buoyed channel with stern anchor ready and berth as space allows. Dues are a bit steep: in 1981 Kr20 up to 2m beam, Kr28 2–2½m, Kr38 2½–3m, then Kr49, 58, 67 and 77 at ½m intervals. But what really shook me was the big concession: stays under two hours are charged at only half price!

The loos and showers are exceptionally good, and shops are nearby. All repairs except for engine or sails, good bathing beaches near the harbour. The harbour itself, however, is very smelly, and there were sinister upwellings near the entrance to the inner harbour, so I certainly wouldn't swim *there*!

Helsingør (Elsinore)
see insets on chart 131

I trust that no yacht from the homeland of William Shakespeare would ever pass this historic town by. Yachts berth in the splendid yacht harbour on the N side of the promontory: there is an inset of the approaches on the chart as well as a still larger-scale plan of the harbour itself. Berth as space permits, green cards. Diesel at the head of the inner harbour's central mole. There are a few alongside moorings near the fuel point, along the SW side of the jetty facing it to the NE, and at the end of the outermost jetty in the Inderhavn: these are for boats over 12m length only. Water at the roots of the jetties.

There is a good chandler, and all repairs are available including a sailmaker called Hamlet Sejl! Excellent shops 300m from harbour office. Cafeteria/bar open 1000–midnight (food until 2200), loos and showers there and also halfway along W mole. All facilities. Dues Kr15 up to 2m beam, then Kr5 for each extra ½m to a maximum of Kr45 (1981).

Kronborg Castle was built 1574–85 and so was still fairly new when *Hamlet* was written in 1602. It is easy to spend a whole day here as there are

An old Danish ketch anchored off the entrance to Hornbaek

not only the historic rooms and interiors, of which the chapel is particularly impressive, but also the Maritime Museum. In the town itself, St Mariae Church and Monastery, St Olaf's Cathedral and the Marienlyst Palace are all worth a visit. There is a veteran railway running to Gilleleje, a magnificent aquarium and some beautiful old houses, notably in Strandgade and Stengade near the S end of the commercial harbour.

Passage note – The Sound

Navigationally speaking the Sound presents few problems, although care has to be taken to keep to the buoyed channels among the shoals between Copenhagen and Malmø, and along the Swedish coast from Malmø to Skanør. Two points are, however, worth making. The first is that in practice ferries do not give way to yachts except in emergency, and the ferry traffic across the Sound, especially between Helsingør and Hälsingborg, is unbelievably heavy. The other point is that in N winds there is a brisk *north-going* current through the Sound, which can kick up quite a sea. This current is even stronger in strong easterlies, when the north-going current can exceed 2 knots in the narrower parts. S winds also produce north-going currents, only slightly weaker than those caused by E winds; and only W winds produce a south-going current, but this is probably the strongest of all – up to 3 knots in the Helsingør narrows. The effects are of course produced by winds that are established, and refer to the general wind over the whole SW Baltic rather than taking account of possible local anomalies.

There are also official traffic separation lanes in the northern part of the Sound, and the rules for using or crossing these should be adhered to. The lanes and directions of flow are clearly shown on all charts.

Kronborg Castle, setting for Shakespeare's 'Hamlet', is one of the most interesting Renaissance buildings in Denmark. There has been a castle on this headland, guarding the entrance of the Sound, since the twelfth century.

Helsingør yacht harbour: Kronborg Castle can be seen in the background

Råå (Hälsingborg) Sweden *see inset on chart 131*

I apologise to the reader (and indeed the printer!) for going back on my normal usage of printing å as aa, but that would make the name of this, the yacht harbour for Hälsingborg, Raaaa!

Visiting yachts should not use the commercial harbour at Hälsingborg. Råå is a large modern marina which is a Customs port and provides all facilities. Diesel (cheaper in Sweden than Denmark in 1981, unlike most commodities) and petrol at the entrance to the yacht harbour, open 0900–1900 every day June 16–Aug 16, shorter hours and closed some days outside this period. The fuel station sells basic foodstuffs; the nearest other shops are 20 minutes' walk. The fuel office will advise on guest berths.

It is also possible on occasion to lie in the old harbour N of the yacht harbour, very much closer to the shops and easier for Hälsingborg. Dues (1981) SKr20.

There is a museum of old boats and fishing opposite the old harbour, and in Hälsingborg itself ($3\frac{1}{2}$ miles) the keep (Kärnan) of the old castle dates from the late fourteenth century and is one of the best preserved mediaeval buildings in Sweden; the Church of St Mary, mid-fifteenth century, is also well worth seeing.

Espergaerde *see plan*

This small harbour is often crowded but is well worth a visit. Yachts lie stern to posts along the S pier as shown, or stern to anchor along the outer half of the N pier, the inner half being reserved for fishermen. Loos and showers at the yacht club, good fresh fish available. Le Part restaurant is considered to be the best between Helsingør and Copenhagen. Dues (1981) Kr30. No fuel.

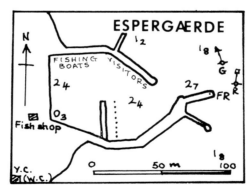

Humlebaek *see plan*

The last relatively unspoiled Danish harbour when one is coming S through the Sound; it can be crowded in the season although there is always room somewhere. Nice atmosphere and pretty surroundings. A yacht yard can do repairs. There are lovely old thatched fishermen's cottages N of the harbour, shops 15 minutes away, two good restaurants. Loos, no showers or fuel.

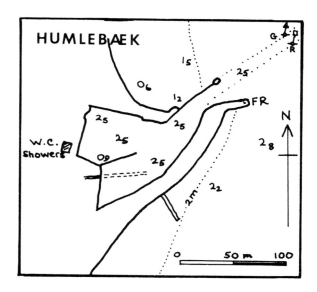

There is a good bathing beach. Do not miss the internationally famous 'Louisiana' museum of modern art. The curious name derives from the fact that the man who built the house married three ladies all called Louise! (One at a time, as far as I know.) It stands in beautiful grounds, and even people who are normally dubious about modern art are pleased that they went.

Alabodarna   Sweden
In spite of its poor showing on chart 131, this harbour hardly rates a plan as it is a simple semicircular basin between two piers. Visitors lie alongside inside the longer NW pier and there is always room; indeed the harbour seems to be little used. Appalling loos at the root of the SE pier. There is an ancient hand-pumped diesel tank which I would avoid except in acute emergency. No shop. Dues (1981) SKr20.

Norreborg, Ven   Sweden
This little harbour is clearly shown on chart 131, as is its entrance from the E, but not the fact that the said entrance is no more than 10m wide. The harbourmaster reckons there is room for 50 yachts, dues (1981) Kr20. Diesel from harbourmaster, water tap, loos, no shower. Bicycles for hire, and well worth it to explore the pretty island: among other things there is a museum of Tycho Brahe, the famous astronomer, near the middle.

Kyrkbacken, Ven   Sweden   *see plan*
Visitors lie alongside the S pier, or to a stern anchor along the N pier and the quay. There is petrol on the quay and a shop at the harbour. Loos, no shower. Bicycles for hire. The old church is worth a visit. Dues (1981) SKr10 up to 9m, SKr15 over. Like all three harbours on this island it is extremely pretty.

Norreborg, my favourite of the Ven harbours

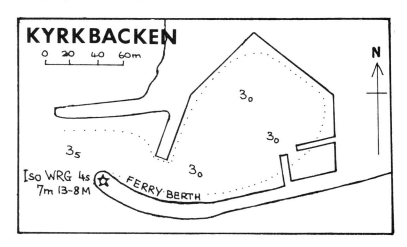

Bäckviken, Ven   Sweden

Another plain semicircular harbour. Yachts lie to a stern anchor with bows to the S pier; the other walls are reserved for the ferry and supply ships. There is a kiosk and (dreadful) loos and, curiously, an occasional bank but no stores. Bicycle hire. Dues (1981) SKr20.

Rungsted

One of several rather similar huge marina developments on the Danish coast of the Sound. Visitors should moor on the face of the central pier and use the intercom (marked GAESTER) to the harbourmaster, who will advise. There are two yacht clubs, one the Royal Danish Y.C., showers, loos, shop, restaurant, fuel, sailmaker, yacht yard. The *kro* beyond Strandvej is a better bet for meals than the clubs. Public transport to Copenhagen, either by bus to Klampenborg and then S–Bane, or walk ¾ mile into town and take the Kystbane, 30 minutes to Copenhagen Central. Altogether a typical huge marina: pretty surroundings and all facilities but not much fun to visit. Dues (1981) Kr30 for 7–11m, Kr45 11–15m; 50 per cent surcharge if left unpaid until someone has to be sent to collect.

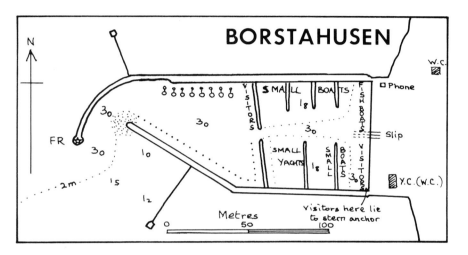

Kyrkbacken, on the Swedish island of Ven

Borstahusen   Sweden   *see plan*
Entering, note the shoal round the end of the S pier, not shown on other
plans but definitely there in 1981. Visitors take a free berth (green card
system), stern to posts along the outer S pier, or may lie bow to quay and
stern to anchor along the inner wall S of the slip. There is a yacht club with
good loo, and also a sauna and shower, though these may be for members
only. Also good loos near the root of the N pier. Shops 150m. Good bathing,
bathing jetty outside the harbour.

Landskrona   Sweden   *see inset on chart 131*
Yachts lie in the first basin to port after the entrance: there is only room for
about six boats with more than 2m beam as the posts are set only just over
2m apart. Water taps, restaurant near harbour. Shops 500m. Dues were not
charged when I was there in 1981.

The Citadel is most impressive from the outside; the inside has been left
empty and so is rather dull.

Vedbaek
Another large marina, crowded and rather noisy because of traffic along the

Landskrona: the Citadel

Vedbaek. Note the fish stakes to the right of the picture.

main coast road. Seas can break right over the N mole, which produces disturbed conditions inside. Fuel and water from the head of the southernmost jetty, loos and showers near root of S pier. Yacht club by root of N pier, loos but no showers. Dues (1981) Kr30. Engineer and sailmaker, no boatyard. Station for trains to Copenhagen, $\frac{1}{2}$ mile away.

Taarbaek   *see plan*
Often overcrowded, but a pretty little harbour: yachts lie stern to anchor as space allows. There is a good restaurant, and a yacht club with good loos but no shower. No fuel. Dues (1981) Kr25 for $2\frac{1}{2}$–3m beam, Kr30 over 3m.

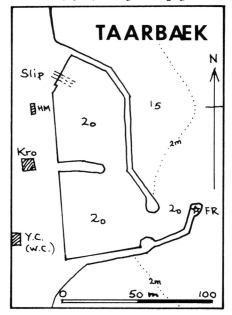

Skovshoved yacht harbour

Skovshoved
Another huge marina development, particularly bleak as there are huge areas of asphalt and then the main coast road before the town begins. Water on jetties, all repairs and facilities, good restaurant in Skovshoved Hotel, two yacht clubs with restaurants. Not very useful for visitors, being too far for convenience from Copenhagen and yet too near to have an individuality of its own. Denmark's largest aquarium is at Charlottenlund, a mile to the S.

Barsebäckshamn   Sweden   *see inset on chart 131*
Almost directly E of Copenhagen and only 9 miles away, this little port could be in a different world, being quiet, rural and apparently miles from anywhere. Approaching, the twin towers of the atomic power station ½ mile S of the entrance are conspicuous. Visitors berth on the inside of the S pier or on the outer face of the central mole, alongside in both cases. The yacht club stands on the central mole, with good loos and a wonderful view over the Sound from the top floor. There are other good loos and showers N of the E corner of the S basin, and an ICA store with all provisions inland from the S basin. No fuel or repairs. Dues (1981) Skr25.

Note the extensive shoal that projects ½ mile out from the land just S of the entrance: the harbour must not be approached until the entrance is bearing S of E. A beacon with a white S cone on shore kept in line with the lighthouse on the N pier (BWVS) leads in safely, and the end of the shoal is marked by a red can buoy. Even so, the local lifeboat coxwain told me that he has to pull several yachts off the spit every season. However, in spite of these perils, easily avoided by merely studying the chart, it is a pleasant little place, and one of my favourites on this coast.

Vikhög   Sweden
A small harbour and mostly very shallow; the pontoons have 1.6m depth at the ends reducing farther in, and the only place for a deeper boat is alongside

the E pier where there is about 2m at mean level. No facilities, and the buoyage was a little eccentric when I was there: the important W cardinal W of the entrance turned out in 1981 to be a white spar buoy with a black S cone rather roughly nailed onto it. A pretty little place, none the less.

Hellerup

This small harbour just N of Tuborg has really very little room, but it is always worth a try as the large Svanemølle marina is only a mile to the S. Have a stern anchor ready before entering. There are showers, loos, sauna, shops, restaurant. Dues (1981) were Kr30 per day for the first three days, but after that very much higher. Good bathing just N of the harbour. Hellerup is also only 500m from the Tuborg brewery where guided tours are available, including tasting session! Denmark's largest aquarium is at Charlottenlund, a mile to the N.

Tuborg

The harbour is owned by the brewery – as you can tell from the pierhead lights, set in replica lager bottles – and should not be entered by yachts.

Copenhagen (København) *see plans*

I will deal below with the individual yacht harbours in Copenhagen, but it may be easier if I summarise their characteristics first, to make the choice easier and also deal with the general information on the town.

A general note first, though: when moving about anywhere in the Copenhagen harbour area the boat should be stowed and secured as for the open sea: wash from tugs, passenger catamarans and hydrofoils can produce motion quite as severe as anything one is likely to encounter in the open. Indeed considerable rolling can be experienced in Langelinie, the traditional yacht harbour for visitors to Copenhagen, where the berths are constantly disturbed by wash from passers-by.

Users of this book should not need the special large-scale chart 134 of Copenhagen as the necessary detail is supplied on the plans provided.

Of the available harbours, Langelinie is far the most central, although even it is a good mile from the city centre. The only berth closer to the city is the 100m or so of Nyhavn, outside the bridge, which yachtsmen are allowed to use by arrangement: this is so central that I would regard it as highly unsafe to leave a boat there unattended. To the N and 2 miles from the city centre, Svanemølle is a large marina with 1300 berths. Skudehavn is much the same distance but has less transport, while Margretheholmshavn, closer as the crow flies, is in the wrong side of the water and so a good 3 miles from the centre by land. Finally, there are the harbours S of the town, generally lumped together as Sydhavnen. These are some 2½ miles from the centre but very much up a blind alley, so they are more useful for someone approaching Copenhagen from the S with the idea of turning back afterwards than for passing through. On the whole I would expect most people to use

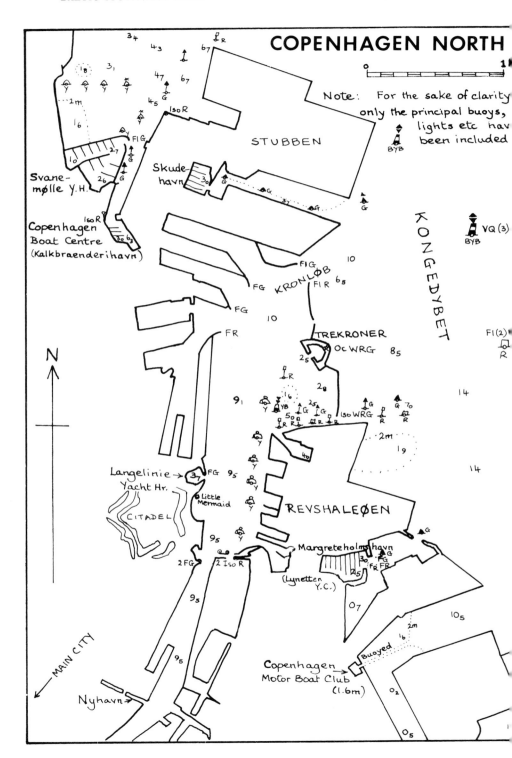

Svanemølle or Langelinie, possibly with a night at Skudehavn or Margretheholmshavn before a morning arrival at Langelinie.

I hardly know where to begin on the subject of things to do and see in Copenhagen: I have been there several times and still find new delights every time. The famous Little Mermaid statue is only a few yards from the Langelinie harbour, and of course it should be seen, but there are many other statues which I find more impressive: how about Sinding's 'Valkyr' on the main road S from Langelinie towards the town centre? If she got in among that lot at Bayreuth she'd soon liven things up! A little farther S in Bredgade is an enchanting little Russian Orthodox church: look for the three onion-shaped golden domes. If there are children or young aboard a visit to the Tivoli is a must: it has fairground amusements, concerts, plays, bands, gardens, and dozens of good restaurants to suit every taste and pocket. The Thorvaldsen Museum, showing the works of this famous sculptor and his private art collection, is another favourite, housed in a splendid Neo-classical building of his own design, and of course there are the castles: Amalienborg, Christiansborg and my favourite Rosenborg, built around 1610 by Christian IV as a country retreat, and still surrounded by parkland. And the churches: the cathedral, modern but splendid, Holmens Church (originally an anchor factory) with wonderful carvings, and over the bridge Our Saviour's Church in Prinsessegade, Christianshav, whose tower has a spiral staircase up the outside. And although you are not allowed in, the Stock Exchange on Børsgade near Christiansborg, must also be seen . . but I could go on forever. The only thing to do is to get one or two of the excellent (and usually free) tourist guides and find out for yourself. But take a pair of comfortable shoes!

Svanemølle
see plan Copenhagen

With its 1300 berths, this was still the biggest marina in Denmark when I was there, although that may no longer be true. There is always room, and all facilities are available at the harbour including a club with loos, showers and restaurant, repairs, sailmaker, fuel and water. Supplies can be bought near the harbour. The railway (S-bane) station is 500m, with frequent trains to the centre of Copenhagen. For those who do not enjoy the hassle of Langelinie, it is one of the best bases from which to explore the city.

Copenhagen Boat Centre
(Kalkbraenderihavnen)
see plan Copenhagen

Just S of Svanemølle, this small harbour has permanently let berths and a few for visitors, but they are really reserved for boats needing repair, fitting of equipment, or other work to be carried out by the group of firms who make up this enterprise. One of their interesting innovations is an underwater window let into the side of a dock, which enables damage to be assessed by eye without the expense of hauling out. All repairs and stores, and good transport to the city, so if you do have the misfortune to need repairs it is at least possible to enjoy yourself while the work is being done.

Skudehavn *see plan Copenhagen*

The harbour lies about ½ mile E of Svanemølle, but is very much closer to Langelinie by water and so can be a useful place to spend a night before going on to Langelinie in the morning, when a berth is far more likely to be available. The surroundings are grimy and industrial, but there is a club with showers and loos and a restaurant. The station is a pretty dreary walk of a mile, and I would not recommend Skudehavn as a base for visiting the city. Dues (1981) Kr20 up to 10m, Kr30 over.

Langelinie *see plan Copenhagen*

This elliptical little yacht basin within walking distance of the city centre is delightfully set in parks and gardens, but it does get very full, and I always find the sensible thing is to spend a night nearby, perhaps at Skudehavn or Margreteholmshavn, and then sail so as to arrive about 9–10 a.m., when some visitors are usually just leaving. Boats lie bow to quay and stern to buoys, and the constant movement due to wash means that moorings must be made up with care and checked regularly. Showers (always cold, in my experience) and loos through unmarked door one door SW of the harbour office. No facilities: shops about a mile. Dues (1981) Kr30 up to 10m, Kr40 over.

Nyhavn *see plan Copenhagen*

Yachts are allowed to moor, if there is room, in the Nyhavn as far in as the bridge: there is room for four to six boats in all. No facilities, and it is exposed to passing drunks and thieves as well as wash from passing ships. Useful for an hour or two but I certainly would not spend a night there without special reasons, or leave a boat unattended.

Margreteholmshavn (Lynetten Y.C.) *see plan Copenhagen*

The new harbour of the Lynetten Y.C., not to be confused by old hands with the old one 600m to the NNW, no longer in use. The entrance is approached from the Kongedyb, and the harbour lies just S of the huge B & W wharf. There is a buoyed approach channel and the basin has 2.5m. This is the newest yacht harbour in the area, and it is an excellent place to spend a night before going to Langelinie in the morning. Showers, water, fuel. There is quite a good bus service to the city (No.8 bus), but it stops running very early so be sure to make enquiries before relying on it for the return trip, as it is a long and expensive taxi ride. Dues in 1981 were a modest Kr20 per boat.

Fiskerhavnen

The approach to this harbour is adequately covered by chart 132: the Kalvebodløb is buoyed, and the guest berths are mostly on the jetties NW of

Langelinie yacht basin, Copenhagen

Nyhavn, the most central mooring in Copenhagen

145

this channel, before it opens out into the Fiskerhavn proper. In all there are 1000 berths here, and it is in a green belt area so quite attractive. There are loos and showers, fuel and buses to the city, or one can walk ¾ mile and take the S-bane. This is a pleasant and convenient base from which to explore Copenhagen, and well worth considering in spite of the detour that is involved if going on.

Hvidovre

This small harbour 1½ miles SW of Fiskerhavn is small and tends to suffer from swell. It has loos, showers and fuel, but there seems no reason for a visitor to prefer it to Fiskerhavn.

Note: The last two harbours have been dealt with out of their normal order because they form part of the Copenhagen complex.

Lomma Sweden

Although this harbour is almost exactly E of Copenhagen, as Lomma lies in a bight and the shoals around Saltholm get in the way it is a sail of some 20 miles.

This is a river-mouth harbour and there is little room for visitors, but they do not turn up very often, I gather. The N pierhead is painted white and is conspicuous: once in, berth along the N wall as space allows; do not approach the S side too closely as there is only 1.5m. Get as far up the river as possible as the facilities are on the S side, so the nearer to the bridge the better. Toilets in the club, and shops are strung along a road running parallel to the S quay about 150m to the S. One of the supermarkets stays open until 2100 every day. Good bathing near the entrance. No dues in 1981.

Malmö Sweden

As with Hälsingborg farther N, yachts are asked not to use this large commercial harbour but to go to Limhamn, effectively the yacht harbour for Malmö.

Kastrup *see plan*

The new yacht harbour is ½ mile N of the commercial harbour, which also has a yacht basin. All three have their own separate entrances, as the plan shows. The new harbour is just as central for shopping as the old one and the facilities are better, so I would recommend it of the two. It has good loos and showers: key from the harbourmaster at the yacht club building, Kr25 deposit. Shops are about ten minutes, as is the bus stop: Nos.9 and 32 go to Copenhagen. The old yacht harbour has poor loos and no showers, but there is a yacht yard, Heller Yachtvaerft, which can do repairs.

Kastrup is within walking distance of Copenhagen Airport, which makes it a very convenient place from which to change crews by air.

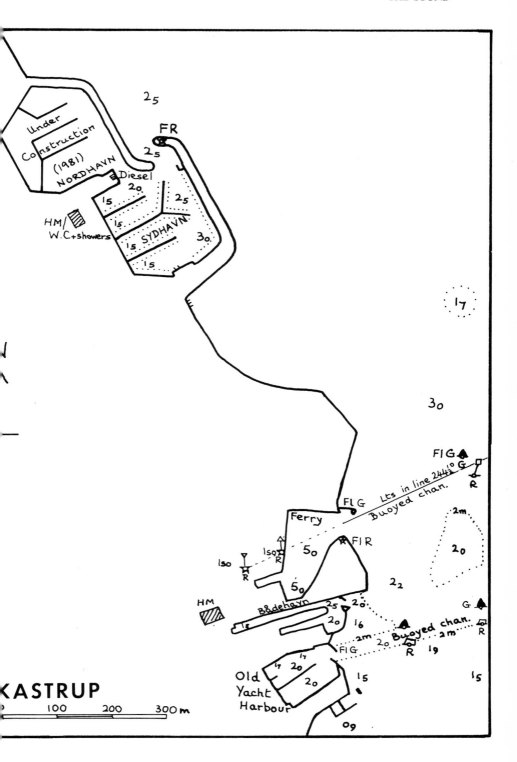

2_5

FR

Under Construction (1981) NORDHAVN

2_5

Diesel

2_0

1_5

2_5

HM/ W.C + showers

1_5

SYDHAVN

1_5

3_0

1_5

1_5

1_7

3_0

FI G

Lts in line 244½° G

R

FI G

Buoyed chan.

$2m$

Ferry

2_0

FI R

5_0

Iso

Iso R

R

2_2

5_0

HM

Bådehavn

2_5

2_0

G

2_0

1_5

1_6

$2m$

Buoyed chan. $2m$

R

FI G

2_0

R

1_9

Old Yacht Harbour

1_7

2_0

1_7

2_0

1_5

1_5

0_9

KASTRUP

0   100   200   300 m

Dragør *see plan*

A highly attractive place in its own right, and as it is only a couple of hours' sail from Copenhagen it is also a possible place to spend a night before sailing to Langelinie. There are also bus connections with Copenhagen, but it is not safe to count on using it as a base for exploring the capital as the berths available are not always suitable for leaving the boat unattended for the whole day.

There are three separate harbours, each with its own entrance, but note that there is 0.6m rise and fall of tide, which means that at average LW the level is already 0.3m below chart datum, and SE winds can lower the water level by up to 1m in prolonged gales. Even at half this figure, the yacht harbour is left looking pretty shallow! The best bet for visitors is therefore usually the main N harbour (the ferry harbour being of course banned to yachts): it is always crowded, but it is large and one can always cram in somewhere, though often alongside two or three other yachts. Diesel and water where marked. There are terrible loos near the N inner basin, or the

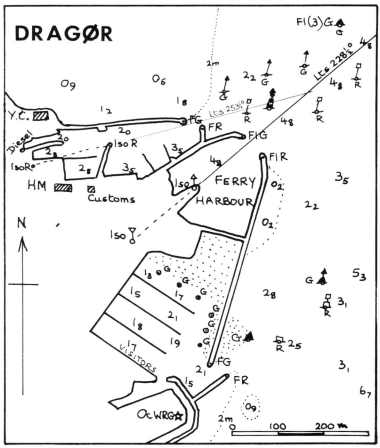

Dragør

key to better ones can be had from the office on payment of dues (Kr25 in 1981). These include nice showers. Fuel is also available in the yacht harbour, which has its own good loos and showers; same dues.

The little town itself is charming and shops are 150m from the old harbour. The museum is worth visiting, if only for a look at the beautiful house (from 1682) in which it is exhibited.

Limhamn Sweden *see inset on chart 132*

This large marina is the yacht harbour for Malmö. It operates the green card system, and I understand that visitors are now charged dues. Visitors' berths are on jetty P, but any green card berth may be used. There are two yacht yards that can undertake repairs, and a fuel jetty (cheaper than Denmark) with a small shop. Other shops 200m.

A useful passage port but not much of interest in the neighborhood of the yacht harbour. Malmö is some 4 miles away but if time allows it is worth visiting. The old part of the town is moated and has a castle and two old churches.

Klagshamn *see plan*

A charming place and well worth a visit, although there are no facilities for visitors and virtually no stores available. Yachts lie in the S basin between posts and short jetties (pretty wobbly, some of them); no green card system so one must not leave the boat unattended without local advice that the berth taken is free. The N basin is shoal, but shallow-draft boats can lie in its S part alongside the smooth-faced part of the dividing mole if there is no berth in the S basin: sound in carefully. Toilets and shower on the beach 5 minutes to the N, also kiosk and phone. The only shop is a baker, 20 minutes' walk. This harbour holds my personal award for the quantity and quality of its pretty girls, mostly wearing bikini bottoms borrowed from their baby sisters, but I can make no guarantees! Good bathing both inside and outside the harbour.

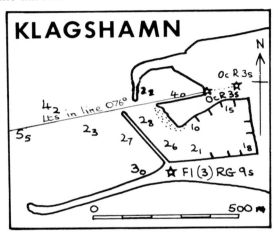

Skanör   Sweden   *see plan*

The last Swedish harbour we shall cover, dealt with here as it is no longer sensible to treat the Sound as a narrow channel where the ports are mentioned as they come abeam: by now it is nearly 20 miles across.

Approaching from the N or NW there are extensive shoals, but they are well buoyed and should present no difficulty except in poor visibility when this would be a dangerous area to sail in, especially as it is impossible to predict the currents accurately. The harbour should be approached from the NW, and it is dangerous to attempt to enter or leave it in winds from W to N over force 6 as severe seas build up on the bar 200m from the entrance. There are conspicuous long white beaches either side of the entrance. The harbour is an uncomfortable place in winds between W and N, when the swell rolls right in, but otherwise it is a pleasant place.

Reasonable showers and loos in red house behind harbour office, no fuel or repairs. Good shops, post office etc about $\frac{3}{4}$ mile away: cross the causeway (deafening cicadas on sunny days) and take the second road to the right, 200m past the windmill. The village has been an important fishing port since 1200 and there are the ruins of a castle near the church at the N end. Good swimming.

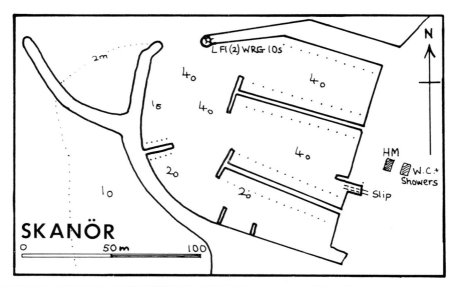

Skanör. The approach is dangerous in strong onshore winds.

Køge Bugt Strandpark:
Brøndby, Vallensbaek, Ishøj and Hundige   *see plan*

Note that the plan of this huge development is very much of the sketch
variety: when I was there in 1981 building was still in progress and the
Danish charts did not even show the existence of these harbours. But this is
one of the most interesting, and in my view praiseworthy, new constructions
anywhere in Europe, and as the approaches to the three entrances are all
pretty straightforward it seemed silly to leave the harbours out, even though
the facilities will no doubt have been increased before this book is published.

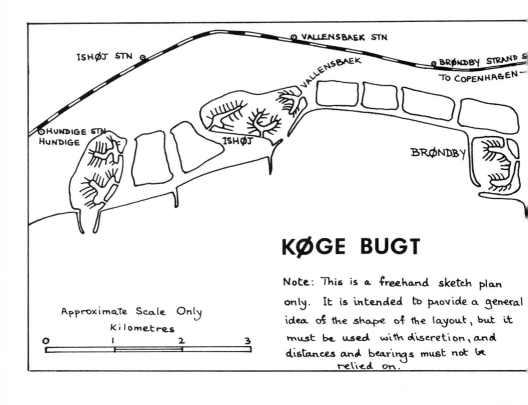

KØGE BUGT

Note: This is a freehand sketch plan only. It is intended to provide a general idea of the shape of the layout, but it must be used with discretion, and distances and bearings must not be relied on.

Approximate Scale Only
Kilometres

Køge Lystbaadehavn. The water tower at the right makes a good landmark, as do the red and green painted pierheads.

All four of the harbours are made up of artificial islands in a lagoon, each island having several yacht jetties. As the islands are intricately shaped a very large number of berths is supplied, but as you can only see the next couple of jetties before a corner intervenes the effect is that of a small harbour. When finished the whole complex will provide 4000 berths, and I have no doubt that each harbour will have wide facilities. When I was there there were already yacht club buildings, water on the jetties, a green card system, showers and loos, and a fuel and chandlery station at Hundige. The trees were only shin-high, but when these have grown and the scars from the earthmovers have disappeared under grass it is going to be something really special. There are S-bane stations about a mile from all the harbours except Brøndby, all are close to a bus service to Copenhagen, and Ishøj and Hundige have beach buses connecting with the stations. So one could easily visit Copenhagen from any of these harbours.

Mosede
see plan

This artificial harbour in Køge Bugt is less crowded now the Strandpark harbours have opened nearby, and it is not much visited by foreigners as it is off the direct course, but if offers a satisfactory berth if needed. There is water on the jetties, loos in the harbour and a yacht club with loos and locker-room showers. Diesel and petrol are available, and there is a kiosk at the harbour and a shop (up to the road and turn right) about 500m away. Dues (1981) were Kr20 up to $2\frac{1}{2}$m beam, plus Kr5 for each extra $\frac{1}{2}$m up to

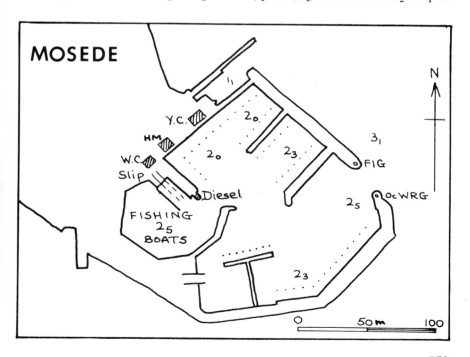

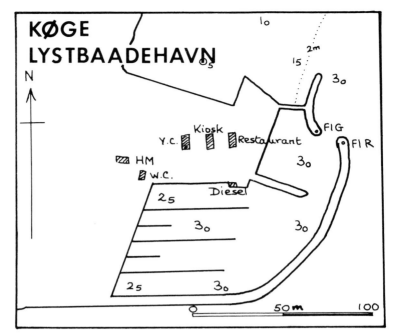

Køge: the old town

Kr 35 maximum. Saturday and Sunday nights spent consecutively were charged as one night plus only Kr5 for the second (the cold wind of competition?).

Køge Lystbaadehavn *see plan*

Note that yachts are no longer allowed in the town harbour. The yacht harbour is particularly easy to identify from seaward as the pierheads are painted red (S) and green (N), at night they are also lit. Berth as space allows (green cards), dues (1981) were Kr25 except alongside the fuel berth (at root of N inner mole) which is normally reserved for large boats and cost Kr50. Restaurant, kiosk and small shop in the harbour, all shops in town 1 mile away. Harbourmaster will lend bicycles free of charge, but beware – the only brakes are of the back-pedal variety which one tends to forget about in a crisis if not used to them (if you read this, madam, may I repeat my apologies!). The HM is very helpful and speaks good English, and this would be a good place to leave a boat for the winter as it is well placed, and yet slightly off the beaten track and therefore cheaper. A winter place out of the water (because of ice) cost Kr700 in 1981: about £50. There would be additional charges of about Kr200 at the beginning and end for the use of the lift, but even so the whole cost would be under £100 at 1981 rates. Sailmaker.

In the town do not miss St Nicolaj Church from around 1324, full of beautiful things including a pulpit from 1624 and altarpiece from 1652. The town also contains Denmark's oldest half-timbered house, which dates from 1527, and many other lovely buildings, mostly in Kirkestraede.

Bøgeskov, a typical pierhead harbour

Stevns Klint, 23 miles S of Copenhagen, will be passed close by on the way from there to Praestø or the Smaalands

Bøgeskov

A usefully placed little pierhead harbour that can be a good passage harbour before or after crossing the Køge Bugt. There are buoys in the approach (see chart 132), and two FR leading lights lead past the entrance at night: one must turn to port and enter when the entrance is abeam, but there are plenty of lights on the walls to show the layout. Berths on the W side of the harbour have 2m, those on the E side 2.2m, but there is 1m tidal rise and fall and SW to W winds can lower the level by up to 0.6m so it is possible to have over 1m less than charted. The harbour is crowded at summer weekends. Dues (1981) Kr25.

There is a small chemical loo at the landward end of the pier, but otherwise no facilities. Quite a good restaurant W of the harbour, and a popular though shallow bathing beach W of the pier. The smell which is sometimes pervasive is rotting seaweed, not sewage! I seem to have made it sound unattractive, but somehow it manages to be a rather charming, odd little place, and it is set in delightful country.

Note: This area and southwards to Stevns Klint and the Smaalands is the worst part of the SW Baltic for fish stakes, and navigation at night without local knowledge is a risky business once one gets into shallow water.

VI · The Waters South of Sjaelland from Stevns Klint including the Smaalands, Fehmarn Belt and some German Harbours

For cruise planning chart and key to harbours covered, see combined chart at the beginning of Section IV, on page 120.

Rødvig   *see plan*

A large and rather expensive harbour, but usefully placed and a good place for shopping. The entrance is well lit and straightforward: the yacht harbour is the E basin. There are poor loos, and two showers so close together that if you do have to share you are going to get to know each other *very* well. Water from hoses, fuel as marked. The harbour shop has fresh bread and a good selection of food, also chandlery, but anything they don't have can probably be found in the village, only 150m, as can two banks. Grill and cafeteria at the harbour, rather dull *kro* up coast road towards Stevns. Boatyard can repair wooden hulls, small sail repairs can be undertaken, and Knud Larsen,

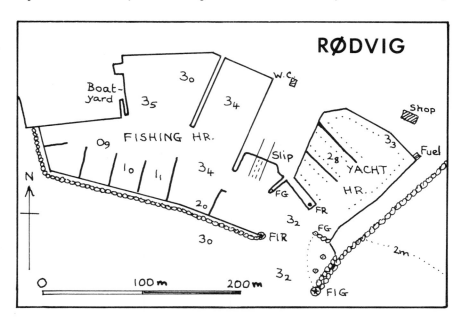

Rødvig

Lund Bro – just to prove I have been there! But I advise against trying it.

Rødvig Motor (Havnevej 18) can do diesel repairs. Dues were rather steep in 1981: Kr40 up to 12m, Kr60 12–25: that was for the first day, subsequent days rather cheaper. I found nothing of great interest in the village.

Lund Bro
This rough stone jetty is engulfed by eel nets, and is almost impossible to reach without local knowledge. Such little room as is available is often fully taken up by local fishing boats. Avoid.

Fakse
A factory with a chimney and two high whitish towers makes a good landmark for this harbour, which provides a good, sheltered harbour of refuge, but otherwise should be avoided. Cement dust swirls in the wind,

158

and there are no facilities whatever. Dues are alleged to be Kr15–45, but I can hardly believe anyone would bother to collect them – or have the nerve! The town, 2½ miles from the harbour, is the home of Denmark's favourite beer for home consumption, Faxe Fad (X has since been abolished from the Danish alphabet).

Praestø

Anyone wishing to visit this charming though rather out of the way town should carry chart 190, which is otherwise unnecessary. I did in fact make my way in there without it, but I had a couple of motor boats to follow: I would not recommend anyone to risk it.

The harbour is protected by islands and shoals and consists of a long quay with projecting jetties, mostly very shallow, and then at the W end an enclosed basin, where visitors should lie, alongside the main harbour wall or on the NW or SW faces of the pier that forms the NE side of the basin. There is a restaurant overlooking the basin, with good loos and showers behind, on the street looking uphill and disguised as ordinary house front doors. Dues (1981) Kr18–35 per day.

There is really good shopping two streets inland, also a good supermarket and baker 300m along the coast road to the WSW of the berths. The town is very pretty with a wide old cobbled street, a lovely square, and interesting old warehouses near the harbour. The fifteenth century church, which has the unusual feature of having two parallel naves, has a splendid altarpiece (1657) by Abel Schrøder the Younger, and a nice rather plain carved pulpit with armorial bearings. There is also a doll and doll's house museum 'Den Lille By', exhibited in a house dating from 1789. Praestø is a long way off the track, but worth it if time allows.

Fakse, perhaps the most depressing harbour in all Denmark

Praestǿ. A favourite of mine. Moor in the small basin shown.

Passage notes – The Smaalands

These narrow waters are well marked and present no problems to the alert navigator, but the large-scale Danish charts (161 and 160 for the main E–W passage, 162 for the Grǿnsund, and 163 and possibly 191 for Guldborg Sund) must be carried as appropriate. Coming from the NE, the first channel is known as the Bǿgestrom and it runs through shoals that run up to 3 miles offshore, so I would not care to try to enter the channel from seaward in bad visibility. Streams can run strongly in the narrow places. All the bridges in the area have a clearance of 26m, except where noted.

Stavreby and Sandvig

These very small harbours at the E end of the Smaalands have respectively 1.6m and 1.7m in the approach and harbour at mean level: W winds reduce this by up to 0.8m, so they are dangerous places to visit because a change of wind can leave you neaped. I tried to enter Sandvig in 1981, drawing 1.2m, but grounded well before reaching the harbour. Only suitable for very shoal draft boats. Both harbours have water and fuel, shops at Sandvig.

Nyord

A pretty little harbour and adequately shown on chart 161. There is 2.2m in the approach channel and a little less inside: the harbourmaster said 1.8–1.9m. W winds lower the level by up to 0.3m. The entrance is little more than 5m wide, but there is plenty of room inside though it becomes crowded in the high season. Good loos and showers, water tap beside. The little island is mostly marsh, but the inhabited W part has the unusual feature of a steep hill: walk up it and you will find just how soft your leg muscles have become in flat Denmark, if you are anything like me! The village has a small store and an ancient (1774) village shop: diesel can be had in cans from either. There is a curious symmetrical octagonal church (1846) with a steeple and a votive ship, and pretty thatched houses, some with the thatch on a tile base. The island is a bird sanctuary and many species can be seen in the marshes NE of the village.

Lindholm
The island houses a research institute studying animal viruses, and landing is forbidden.

Stege
see plan

This splendid old town is unfortunately rather dominated by the sugar factory, and if the wind is in the SW the smell can be quite powerful until one gets used to it. But it is still well worth a visit.

The approach is by a long buoyed channel but, as the chart shows, for an average yacht there is plenty of room out of the channel in most places. There is also a short-cut from Nyord to Stege via the Nordre Løb, quite easy

Nyord: breathe in when passing through the entrance

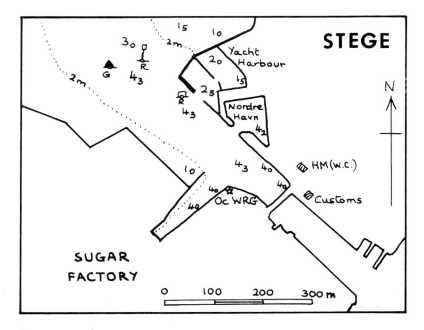

to find in good visibility.

If there is no room in the Lystbaadehavn, visitors may berth alongside in the Nordhavn (S of the Lystbaadehavn), where there is always room; boats over 9m must use the Nordhavn in any case. Small diesel tank at S side of Lystbaadehavn, and water hoses. Harbour offfce and (nasty) loos just before the bridge. A W gale veering northerly can produce strong in-going stream: otherwise the stream goes with the tide (o.4m mean range). Dues in 1981 were very complex: examples are Kr32 for 7–8m, Kr35 9–10m, Kr43 11–12m.

The shops are very good and only 150m from the berths. The town still has its mediaeval ramparts and moat, and the splendid town gate (Storegade) should be seen, with the Møn museum next door. The church of St Hans should also be visited: dating from the early thirteenth century, it has some perfectly charming fifteenth century frescoes.

Kalvehave   *see plan*

In recent years the harbour has been hugely improved and is now one of the best in the area, although it is still subject to unpleasant swell in strong SW winds.

Visitors mostly berth alongside the N and E walls of the old harbour (the E basin), although vacant berths in either harbour can also be used. Diesel pump on the inner wall of the old harbour, just E of the slip; service from the chandler about 100m to the N. Excellent small supermarket about the same distance but NW: exceptional showers and loos in harbour office complex. Hotel. I have never visited the church which lies about a mile to the W, but it looks very beautiful from the water. Dues (1981) Kr20 for 6–8m, Kr25 8–10m, Kr28 10–12m, Kr33 over.

Note that the direction of lateral buoyage changes at Kalvehave Bridge.

Petersvaerft Bro
This idyllic jetty mooring is owned by a timber firm, and it is only available for visitors from June 15 to August 1. There is 2m depth at the end of the jetty but much less at the sides. Unsafe in strong winds, but a charming place for a picnic or a night in settled weather. Water tap, no other facilities.

Vordingborg Nordhavn   *see plan*
The harbour is subject to silting and whenever I go there there seems to be less water than on the chart: in any case winds between E and SW can lower the water level by up to 1m. There is more water on the town quay W of the yacht jetties, however, and most yachts will find enough water there in any conditions even if there is not enough at the jetties. The mud is fairly thin and it is often possible to haul in to a berth when technically aground! Dues (1981) Kr26 up to 10m, Kr40 over.

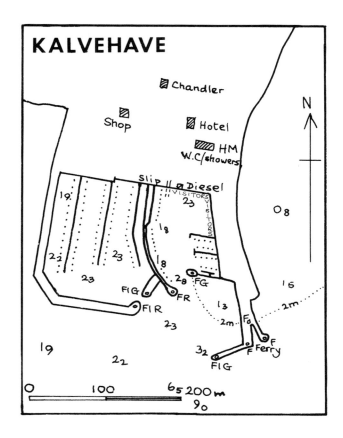

VORDINGBORG NORDHAVN

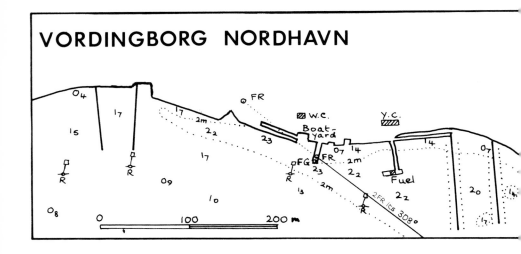

There is water on the jetties, and fuel on the short jetty at the W of the yacht harbour. Repairs can be done and there is a sailmaker. First-class shopping 10 minutes from the berths. The town is dominated by the Goose Tower (Gaasetaarnet) built by Valdemar Atterdag in the 1360s and the view from the top on a clear day is remarkable. There are also ruined twelfth century fortifications, and a most beautiful church, founded by the same Valdemar, with splendid frescoes, an altarpiece from 1641 and a lovely hanging pulpit from 1601.

Vordingborg Sydhavn
This small harbour ESE of the Masnedsund Bridge has little room for visitors and is disturbed by wash from passing traffic. I can see little reason why any visitor should prefer it to the Nordhavn, except perhaps when depth is critical, as there is 3m in the entrance, although this quickly falls to 2m once inside. Not recommended.

Karrebaeksminde   *see plan*
Rather off the normal cruising tracks, and there does not really seem to be much incentive to make the detour although it is a pleasant enough little place. The approach requires care, especially from the S, and the entrance and outer harbour can be extremely rough in strong onshore winds. The only landmark from seaward is a group of red roofs between woods.

The comfortable place to lie is in the inner yacht harbour, through the bridge, but note that this opens only on the hour, and only between ½ hour before sunrise and ½ hour after sunset, with a limit of 0500 to 2100. If late, or with time to wait for the bridge, there is an outer yacht harbour along the S breakwater. This is sheltered enough inside, but if the stream is running strongly it can be very tricky to enter. It is first vital to estimate the speed of

the stream: this is affected by both wind and tide and can attain 4 knots.
When the bridge does open, the signals are: 1 FR for no passage, 2 FR
permits passage E to W, 3 FR for passage W to E. Berth in the inner marina
as space allows. Dues (1981) Kr25.

There are showers and loos in the yacht club near the inner marina; they
open at 0700 every day and the club itself at 1000. There is a good
supermarket 100m N of the harbour, and a baker on the S side between
outer and inner yacht harbours, also a vegetable and fruit stall and several
fish shops and smokeries. Meals can be had in the yacht club. The club dog,
by the way, looks ferocious but is soppy!

*Karrebaeksminde. The entrance to the outer yacht basin is visible at right
centre.*

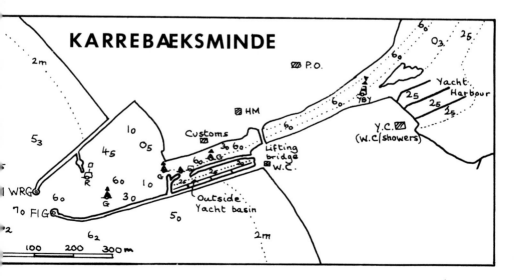

Naestved

It is possible to sail up a buoyed channel which becomes a canal from Karrebaeksminde to Naestved, and having come so far it would seem a pity not to. Visitors can lie in either of the basins at the extreme end of the canal, close to the town centre and first-class shops. Motor repairs available, also diesel, water etc. The two churches are both worth seeing: St Peter's, mainly from 1375 with good frescoes, including one of Valdemar Atterdag and his queen, and St Morten, with a great wooden triptych by Abel Schrøder the Younger. The Town Hall, begun in 1450, is also beautiful though the inside is not open to the public, and the Helligsandhuset (Holy Ghost House), a mediaeval hospital, now houses an interesting museum.

The palace on Gavnø, the main island in the lagoon between Karrebaeksminde and Naestved, dates from 1755 and is on the site of a convent founded by Queen Margrethe I in 1402. Gardens, large art collection and beautiful carvings by Abel Schrøder in the abbey church. It is possible to anchor off the NE corner of the island and row down to the village (½ mile), or visit from Naestved (3 miles). Open 10–5 in summer.

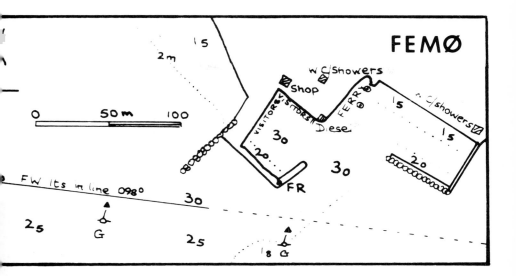

Femø
see plan

The greatest care is needed navigating among the islands in this part of the Smaalands, but the numerous shoals are all well marked and the alert navigator should experience no difficulty. The approach to this island has 3m depth, as does the W basin; the E one has a good deal less. S winds can lower the mean level by up to 1.5m, and there is a mean tidal range of 0.6m.

Visitors mostly berth in the old W basin alongside the NW and NE walls: be sure to leave the ferry room to manoeuvre. Diesel where marked, service from the small Oceka shop. Good loos and showers. The island is flat but pretty, the town a good mile away. The new basin is subject to swell in strong W to SW winds. Dues (1981) Kr30 for 7–9m, Kr45 9–12m.

Askø

This small pierhead harbour has 2.2m depth in the W part where visitors may berth, the deeper E side being reserved for the ferry. SE to SW winds can lower the mean level by up to 1m, and there is a 0.4m mean tidal range. Enter with care, as it is necessary to turn to port between two dolphins, placed there to assist the ferry. There is a quite reasonable loo, and a water hose NE of the ferry berth.

The village is a full mile away, and has a good shop which is shut Wednesdays and Sundays, and closes early on Saturdays. It has a pretty church with an ancient ship painting, a votive model ship, and a good old altarpiece, crucifix and painted pulpit: enquire at the shop where to ask for the key. The island is full of orchards and there are wild sweet plums in the hedges. The poplar windbreaks are reminiscent of Normandy.

Bandholm, Lolland
see inset on chart 160

Near the beginning of the buoyed channel that leads to Sakskøbing, and an interesting and unusual harbour. The approach channel runs close past the heavily wooded islet of Havneø, which I have found useful in providing a perfect lee for striking sail: it would fulfil this function in strong winds from anywhere between SW and N.

Visitors berth alongside the NW quay, or in the outer harbour if there is a slot free. Water hose near the root of the SE pier; luxury loos and showers in the red building at the W corner of the harbour are open only 0800–1900, all-night ones at the head of the NW mole. Dues (1981) were Kr35 up to 10m, Kr45 10–12m, Kr55 over.

The village is very pleasant, with some good old warehouses, and Knuthenborg Park ($\frac{3}{4}$ mile up a beautiful poplar avenue) is a large safari park with all manner of animals, woods and rare trees. There is also a veteran steam railway which runs to Maribo on Saturdays and Sundays: it has engines going back to 1879, and one passenger coach ten years older than that. Shops (general store and baker) are down the main road 800m SW of the harbour.

Sakskøbing
see inset on chart 160

A handsome old town lying at the end of a fjord about 3 miles long, itself approached by a buoyed channel another $4\frac{1}{2}$ miles long. The fjord part is

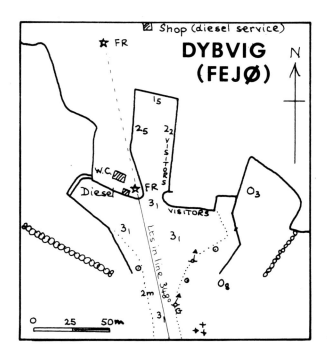

extremely pretty. Note that the large posts stuck around the first narrow part of the fjord and elsewhere have small pieces of red or green plastic (where they have not fallen off) nailed to them to show which side they should be passed: they are in any case well shown on the chart.

Visitors berth alongside as space allows; there is usually plenty of room but it can become crowded if there are a couple of big ships in. The harbourmaster is helpful and speaks good English.

The truly awful loos (perhaps the worst I saw) are on the SW quay. The nearest shop is only 50m away and the main shopping street no more than 100m, so it is a most convenient place for heavy shopping. There is a highly elegant church, built about 1300, with a gilt altarpiece from Lübeck (1500) and a very nice mid-sixteenth century carved pulpit, also a fourteenth century crucifix and a votive ship.

Dybvig, Fejø   *see plan*
This is very much the larger of the two harbours on this island. Visitors can lie on the wall E of the entrance to the inner basin, or on either side wall of that basin. SW winds can lower the mean level by up to 1m. Loos and antique shower near the head of the W mole; also diesel pump, served from the shop 100m N of the harbour. Diesel is sold only 0800–1730. A pretty, pastoral island.

Vesterby, Fejø
The small harbour is shoal on the SE side and the central part is reserved for the ferry, which leaves very little room for visitors. There are loos, a shop and a *kro*.

Kragenaes, Lolland   *see plan*
The three green buoys should be left close to starboard in approaching this harbour as the water is shoal S of the line: there are leading beacons which give the correct angle of approach.

Berth as space allows: there is usually a free slot. Water on the jetties, small yacht club with good loo and shower. There is a shop only 50m from the harbour up the one road; farther on (500m) is the Happy-Naes Kro (only a Dane would name a pub with a pun in a foreign language!) which has a good restaurant. Otherwise there is no real village, but it is a pretty area.

Vejrø   *see plan*
This large new yacht harbour was still being built when I was there in 1981, and the plan should be used with caution as it is partly based on what were predictions. It was all beautiful, new and empty, but I am sure that there will be good facilities by the time this book is published. Even then there was a small loo, with water tap, and shower. There is no village on the island, just scattered farms, but one of those had a beer sign on its wall and is probably a bar/cafe in the season. (I was there in late August, when all good Danish

yachtsmen seem to be laid up, which is a pity as it is often the best weather of the year.) It will probably never be a place for stocking up, but a nice quiet harbour for an overnight stop.

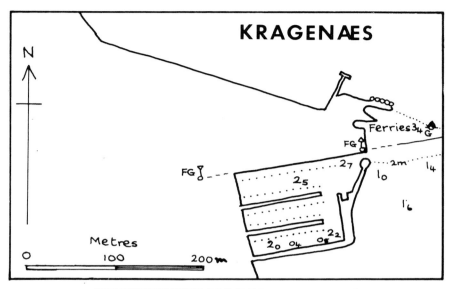

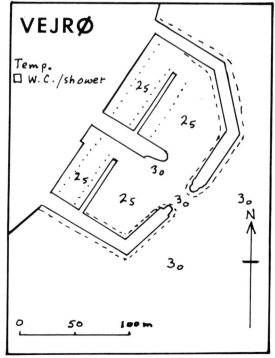

Passage note – Smaalands southwards to the open sea

That concludes the main westward passage through the Smaalands, as the next harbours to the W, Onsevig and Omø, were dealt with under the Store Baelt (Section III). However, there are two sounds leading S from the Smaalands into the Mecklenburg Bugt: the Grønsund to the E, and the Guldborg Sund to the W. There is also the outside passage via Klintholm and Gedser: this needs no particular comment as it is perfectly straightforward, and is less used by yachtsmen as it is exposed, and rather dull compared to the Smaalands. These harbours are dealt with below on an E to W basis, with the two sounds being covered N to S.

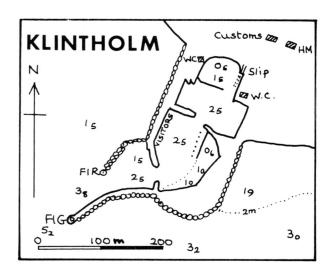

Klintholm, Møn *see plan*

For anyone choosing the outer passage S of the islands of Møn, Falster and Lolland this is an important harbour, but the outer basin is most uncomfortable in winds between S and SW and there is often no room further in. The harbour has good loos and showers, water on the jetties, and diesel and petrol are available. Dues alter with every metre of length: examples (1981) were Kr33 for 8–9m, Kr35 9–10m, and Kr40 10–11m. A most useful passage port. Strong walkers can reach the beautiful cliffs, the highest in Denmark, of Møns Klint some 3 miles to the E.

GRØNSUND HARBOURS FROM THE NORTH

Stubbekøbing, Falster *see inset on chart 162*

The yacht harbour lies E of the main harbour: note that the S parts are shoal. There are nice loos and a small hand-shower at the SW corner of the yacht harbour, and some chandlery and charts at the BP station S of the ferry

berth. Reasonable shopping near the church, about 10 minutes from the harbour. The church here is one of my favourites: dark and heavily pillared with a baroque pulpit and beautiful fresco decorations, especially in the main side-chapel. The organ loft is also rather fine, and the altarpiece is interesting though consisting mostly of text. The town also has the largest Motorcycle Museum in northern Europe at Nykøbingvej 52. Dues (1981) Kr25 for 7–10m, Kr30 10–15m.

Bogø

The approach for this small harbour is clearly shown on chart 162. Yachts berth in the small basin E of the main central mole, the W basin being reserved for the ferry. Only room for a maximum of 10 yachts. In spite of its name the loos are small and horrid, and the only shop is a mile from the harbour. There is a nicely restored windmill near the harbour, but otherwise the island has a rather suburban feel since it has been connected to Møn and thence to Sjaelland by bridges.

Haarbolle Fiskerihavn, Møn

This small basin has 2.5m depth throughout. It tends to be absolutely full on Saturdays and Sundays, as it is the headquarters of a hire fleet, but empty on weekdays. Diesel and motor repairs available. Shop 100m from the harbour, with fresh bread in the mornings. Nice loos and showers. There is a small fisherman's pub, the Skipperkro, but otherwise little in the way of a village. Dues (1981) included Kr33 for 8–9m and Kr40 10–11m. Useful passage port.

Stubbekøbing

The white chalk cliffs of Møns Klint rise to 420ft above the sea, with green beech-clad ravines. A beautiful footpath leads along the wooded clifftops. (See entry on Klintholm.)

173

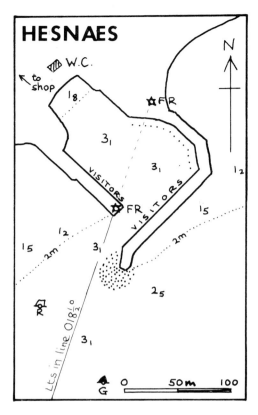

Hesnaes *see plan*

On the open coast of Falster between the Grønsund and Guldborg Sund, this is another vital passage port for anyone on the outer passage. The harbour is shown clearly enough on chart 162, but a plan is given here as that chart is not otherwise necessary except for those using the Grønsund. Note the shoal area around the E pierhead, and beware of extensive fishnets all round the approach.

Visitors moor inside the E pier or the outer part of the W pier, plenty of room alongside usually. Note that there is only 1.8m at the head of the harbour, which with a tide range of 0.9m leaves little enough without allowing for the fact that SW winds can lower the mean level by up to 1.5m: in extreme conditions there is only 1.2m even in the outer, deep part of the harbour. There are rather nasty loos and no showers, but the village 100m to the N is charming with a reasonable small shop and unusual cottages with thatched roofs and reed-covered walls.

Gedser Lystbaadehavn *see plan*

Note that this harbour is ½ mile N of Kroghage Point: the old Gedser harbour E of the point is no longer open to yachts except in emergency. It has its own plan on chart 186, but this does not include the yacht harbour, which is also too far S to get onto chart 163. The plan on 186 should, however, be used if rounding Kroghage Point, where the deep water is close in: once round, keep no more than 1 cable offshore until the yacht harbour entrance is abeam. There is an uncharted radar tower just beside the daymark on Gedser Point, SE of the old harbour: it is 40–50m high and can be seen very much farther than the daymark.

The yacht harbour has luxury loos and showers, a restaurant (Marinakroen) open 1200–2300, and diesel and petrol from fuel berth at the S side of the harbour, as shown on the plan. Small shop 400m: go up to the main road and turn right. Other shops, banks etc $\frac{1}{4}$ mile farther on. Dues (1981) Kr40 for 7–10m, Kr50 10–12m. This is the southernmost harbour in Denmark, on about the same latitude as Middlesborough or the Lake District.

Passage note – Guldborg Sound

Approach from the N presents no difficulties, but coming from the S requires a little care especially if chart 191 (which I find unnecessary) is not aboard. The trick is to keep well in to the Falster side, which is steep-to, perhaps $\frac{1}{2}$ mile off until the S point of Lolland is nearly abeam to port, and then close the Falster shore to 2 cables until the first red buoy of the channel is seen as marked on chart 163 (54°40.2′N, 11°52.1′E). From here there are no problems, but the buoyed channel must be strictly followed.

Hesnaes. These moorings are afflicted by a nasty swell.

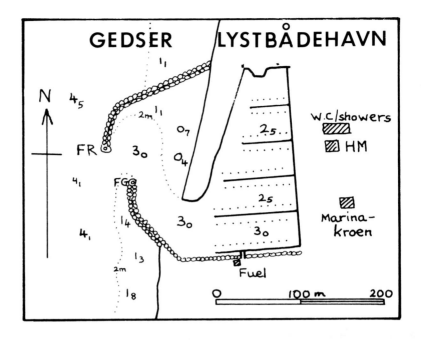

Gedser Lystbaadehavn entrance, in force 7

Guldborg Bridge

A normal opening bridge which opens on demand (usual signals) in daylight hours. Night opening can only be secured with advance notice and on payment of a fee. There is a pier on the W bank S of the bridge with two jetties extending SW from near its head. Yachts can lie here or on the N-facing part of the pierhead, stern to piles. The berths are surprisingly well sheltered from weather but subject to some disturbance by wash from passing ships. There are loos and showers and a shop nearby. Dues (1981) Kr25.

Nykøbing, Falster   *see inset on chart 163*

The third and last of our Nykøbings, and a worthy representative of the clan. There is an opening bridge at the S end of the town: during the summer it will open on demand (usual signals) 0600–1200 and 1300–1800. If caught by this rather early closing time, there is a small yacht jetty about ½ mile SE of the bridge where one can lie until morning in perfect safety, though without many facilities. There is also a new yacht harbour on the W bank just N of the bridge: I have not visited this, as it would be a very long hike into the main town, which is on the E side.

The main yacht harbour is the N part of the basin shown near the N extremity of the chart inset. The yacht club is on the built-up part of the pier at the W corner of the basin: a short jetty projects E from there (not shown on the inset in the 1981 edition of the chart) and guest berths are on that jetty. Otherwise take any free slot (green card system), or it is possible to lie alongside in the Nordhavn at the S end of the basin.

Water on the jetties, loos at club, showers at root of N pier. Dues (1981) Kr25. Gøther Marine is a chandler with charts and repair facilities, just across the road from the E corner of the yacht harbour. Diesel from pump at the NE corner of the broad pier forming the S side of the entrance, service from *skibsproviant* store called Osvaldo's about 300m to the SSE, some 100m beyond the harbour office. It is open 8–4 weekdays, 8–12 Saturdays. There is a supermarket 5 minutes from the yacht harbour, and full and excellent shopping only a little farther.

Nykøbing is a delightful town, and it is a pity that it is relatively seldom visited by foreign yachtsmen because of being off any direct route: I think it is well worth turning aside for. The Gothic church, once part of a monastery, is splendid, with a beautiful baroque pulpit (the only time I have ever seen Moses acting as a caryatid!), a splendid rather restrained altarpiece, and an illustrated family tree of Queen Sophia in an unusual double-topped frame built to fit the vaulting of the church. There is a painting by Lucas Cranach the Elder, and outside is a famous garden of medicinal herbs which I found most interesting. The museum is also worth seeing, housed in 'The Tsar's House' (1700), so called because Peter the Great stayed there in 1716.

Nysted, Lolland

Chart 191 is needed if visiting this port, and it must be up to date as the offshore sands shift. The approach is from the S by a buoyed channel through the Rødsand, the first buoy lying some 7 miles W of Kroghage Point, or if already inside the Rødsand one can cut into the channel by passing close S of the S cardinal buoy marking the SE corner of Flinthorne

Aalholm Castle near Nysted was often raided from the German coast during the Middle Ages, and was defended by a wide deep moat. This tower is the oldest part remaining; much else has been rebuilt and renovated at various periods. Park and castle open daily 10–4 in summer.

Rev, and then steering for the E cardinal buoy a mile SW of Flinthorne Odde. From close E of this steer N into the buoyed channel.

However, I do not really recommend the harbour. There is 3m depth at the heads of the jetties, but only 1m near the roots, and the harbour is exposed to S winds. Furthermore there is 1.5m of tide and WNW gales can lower the mean level by up to 1.5m, so in extreme conditions there can be 2.2m less than charted. Moor at the jetty heads or in front of the harbour office. Dues (1981) Kr35. Showers and loos, water on the jetties, diesel pump. Good shopping close to the harbour.

Don't miss Aalholm Castle, dating back to the twelfth century, and the large veteran car museum at Stubberupgaard, ½ mile W from the castle or a mile from the town centre. The latter also has a huge model railway, and a veteran steam train that runs down to the beach. From a tourist point of view it is an interesting place, but only go there in settled weather.

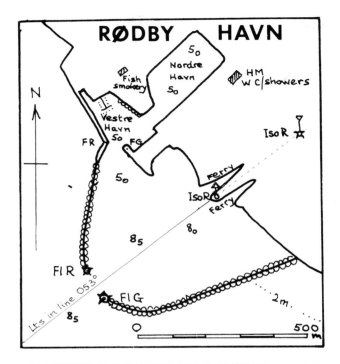

Rødby Havn is more useful than ornamental!

R∮dby Havn   *see plan*

The last of our Danish harbours, and regrettably one of the least attractive, though usefully placed only 10 miles from the German island of Fehmarn. If approaching from the S the harbour can readily be identified by two large buildings, the only ones visible for several miles of otherwise featureless coast. Look out for heavy ferry and commercial traffic including many cruise ships both outside and in the harbour.

There are a few rickety bow and post moorings in the Vestrehavn, or visitors can moor alongside near the NE corner of the Nordrehavn: consult the harbourmaster as soon as possible. There are (poor) loos in the harbour building, and a shower in the office part. Reasonable shops 200m NE from office, large and expensive-looking hotel 100m. There is a very good fish smokery on the road from the Vestrehavn to the harbour office and town.

Do remember that large ships are constantly arriving and departing, and keep a sharp lookout when moving about, entering or leaving. They move silently and cannot alter their manoeuvres once they are committed to them.

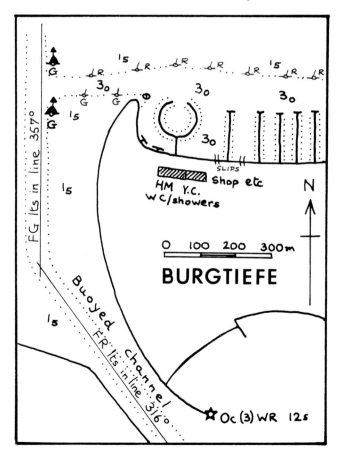

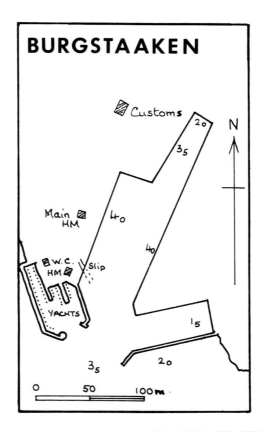

GERMAN HARBOURS ON AND SOUTH OF FEHMARN

The notes given below are in no sense intended to cover the whole of the W German coast, but apart from the fact that I consider that Heiligenhafen is well worth a visit in its own right, it and the Fehmarn ports can be extremely useful if wishing to cross back to the mainland in heavy weather from the NW. In fact, in a NW gale I once had a most comfortable crossing from Rødby Havn down past the SE corner of Fehmarn, and turning W found myself immediately in perfect shelter from both wind and sea.

Burgtiefe *see plan*
Approached from the E, the S coast of Fehmarn is fairly steep-to and using chart 185 it is safe to run along the coast $\frac{1}{2}$ mile offshore until the buoys of the channel are identified. If German Customs clearance is required it is necessary to proceed N to Burgstaaken.

This large marina and holiday development has all possible facilities, including a mobile fibreglass repair service. There are 68 guest berths, and green card berths are also available to visitors, so there is always plenty of room. The official guest berths are on the E side of the nearly circular

181

pontoon at the W side of the harbour. Good loos and showers, diesel and petrol. Good shop, open Sundays in summer as well as weekdays, five restaurants, chandlery. A good place to leave a boat for the winter. Dues (1981) based on length × breadth in metres (quadratmeter): DM10 up to 20, DM12 for 20–30, DM15 30–40, DM23 40–50. Beware the dreaded launderette machine near the harbour office: it takes an unbelievable $1\frac{1}{2}$ hours to do one wash, and then there are no tumble driers.

There is no real town: this is a modern development on what previously was just a sandbar. But a useful passage port.

Burgstaaken   *see plan*
Approached up a well buoyed channel past Burgtiefe, which can easily be seen from the open Fehmarnsund. This is a good place to clear Customs coming back from Denmark. The small yacht harbour is on the W side of the entrance to the main basin. Green card system; if no room one can always squeeze in somewhere in the main harbour. Dues in 1981: DM (length in metres × 2). Petrol and diesel alongside, water on pontoons. Good shop 200m from harbour, also seamen's pub serving respectable meals at reasonable prices by German standards. Charts and duty-free stores available. The main town is a good mile away, but worth a visit.

Heiligenhafen   *see plan*
A charming place and well worth a visit even if not driven there by bad weather. The entrance is safe even in NW gales as long as visibility is good. If approaching from the E in strong westerlies, be prepared for severe seas under and near the bridge that connects Fehmarn with the mainland. From the N a useful landmark is a high tower on the skyline, with an out-jutting

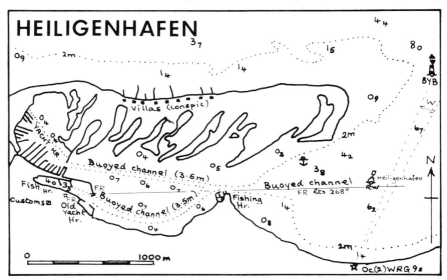

Part of the huge new marina at Heiligenhafen

circular storey near its top. It is almost directly above the main lighthouse, which cannot be seen until much closer in. The row of villas extending almost to the E end of Graswarder is conspicuous and helps orientation (see plan). The ends of the yacht harbour piers are floodlit at night, and FR leading lights and the sectored main light make a night approach easy.

Visitors berth in the main, W yacht harbour: come alongside the first pontoon and a harbour official will be there and will allot a berth. Water at all berths, diesel in the fish harbour closed weekends. Excellent showers and loos (deposit for key), all facilities. The town is only 100m away: good shops and an attractive church.

Glossary of Useful Danish Words

As explained in the Introduction, attempts to use Danish in speech are likely to founder on pronunciation difficulties. These words are designed to help with the understanding of charts, notices, pilot books etc.

Afmaerket	Buoyed, marked	Havnefoged	Harbourmaster
Anker(plads)	Anchor(age)	Havnekontor	Harbour office
Baad	Boat	Hoved	Headland
Baake	Beacon	Klint	Cliff(s)
Bad	Bath, shower	Købmand	Grocer, general store
Bane(gaard)	Railway (Station)	Kontor	Office
Bedding	Slip	Kro	Pub, inn
Bøje	Buoy	Kuling	Wind force 6–8
Braendstof	Fuel	Liggeplads	Berth
Bro	Bridge, jetty	Lille	Small, little
Bruse(bad)	Shower(bath)	Løb	Channel
Bugt	Bight, bay	Lystbaade	Pleasure boat, yacht
By	Town, city		
Dyb	Deep, deep channel	Naes	Point
		Nord (N)	North
Dybde	Depth	Ø	Island, islet
Faerge	Ferry	Odde	Point
Farvand	Fairway, channel	Øst (Ø)	East
		Paelle	Posts
Flak	Shoal	Radiofyr	Radiobeacon
Fyr	Light(house)	Rende	Dredged channel
Gaeste(plads)	Guest (mooring)	Rev	Reef, shoal
		Rolig	Peaceful, quiet
Grund	Shoal	Segl(mager)	Sail(maker)
Haekanker	Stern anchor	Skibsproviant	Ship supplier
Hastighed	Speed	Søkort	(Sea) chart
Havn	Harbour	Store	Great, big

Storm	Wind force 9–10	Tønde	Buoy
Strøm	Current, stream (also electricity)	Tysk(land)	German(y)
		Urolig	Restless, disturbed
Sund	Sound (between shores)	Vaerft	Shipyard, boatyard
		Vaerksted	Workshop
Syd (S)	South	Vand	Water
Told(kontor)	Customs (office)	Vest (V)	West
		Vig	Natural harbour

Note Some official works including *Den Danske Havnelods* use the abbreviations E and W for east and west.

Notes and Corrections

APPROXIMATE MILEAGES BETWEEN PORTS BY THE SHORTEST AVAILABLE NAVIGABLE ROUTE

```
174 102 135  97  64 101 115  77  85 121  66  93  55  50 147  50  90 250  Vordingborg
 76 178 142 233 210 216 145 279 188 178 192 281 238 210 204 232 258       Thyborøn
189 105 102  30 174  49 128  60 168 145 108  45 170  75 171 140            Sønderborg
156 131 108 146  24 151 110 113  86 115 143  25 100 112                    Skanör
128  91  74 143  93 121  72 162  70  26  94 170  75 114                    Roskilde
134  66 106  64 130  62  76  68 109  88  39  73 120                        Nyborg
162 139 116 170  33 166 119 121  51  96 140 148                           Køge
205 143 171  64  71  89 146 175 144 100                                    Kiel
115  48  75  71  48  55  33  89  68                                        Kalundborg
102  65  48 117  95  46  88  44                                            Hundested
113  88  65 138  21 117  68 144                                            Helsingør (Elsinore)
192 130 158  74 123  99 134                                                Heiligenhafen
 67  48  27 102  88  82                                                     Grenaa
115  56  53  25 136                                                         Fredericia
135 108  86 160                                                             Copenhagen (København)
160  78 122                                                                 Assens
 66  65                                                                     Anholt
105                                                                         Aarhus
                                                                            Aalborg
```

Note   This table is designed as an aid to cruise planning, but it must always be borne in mind that these are the shortest distances between the ports concerned. Thus the shortest way from Kalundborg to Vordingborg is (as shown) 66 miles, passing W and S of Sjaelland. The same trip via Copenhagen, going round the other side of the island, is 174 miles. So if going to one place via another it is important to add the distances between the intermediate ports together to arrive at the distance by the particular route chosen.

Index

An anglicised version of the Scandinavian alphabet has been used in this index. Readers are advised to consult the note on the differences between the Scandinavian and West European alphabets, and the usage in this book, on pages 18–19.